This is a story of redemption. ⸺ ⸺⸺ book, told with vulnerability, honesty, and hope, you will see the power of God's grace at work in a life that was broken and pain-filled. You will experience the gentle hand of the Savior leading Susan on a journey to wholeness, into a future of purpose and destiny, and you will be encouraged in your own journey.

—JANE HANSEN HOYT
PRESIDENT/CEO, AGLOW INTERNATIONAL

What a power-packed message of the power of God's love! This is one of the most compelling books I've ever read. The underlying theme is what a difference just one touch from our heavenly Father can make in our lives. Thank you for being obedient to "birth" the vision God gave you. It has the potential to transform the lives of men, women, boys, and girls all over the world. Cindy and I commit to partner with you as you share the power of "One Touch." May He enlarge your territory!

—CARL W. RICHARD, MA
DIRECTOR, ONE FAMILY COUNSELING CENTER
FREE CHAPEL WORSHIP CENTER, GAINSVILLE, GA

I took Susan's manuscript with me on a quick trip to Houston. On the way home, Sunday afternoon, I took it out of the package and started reading. I could not stop. I read straight through as fast as I could shuffle the pages. It is a captivating story! I realize now that as I had sat across from Susan at Copeland's restaurant that day, I was looking into the reality of grace on display. Her story touched me deeply. I realized afresh how marvelous God's grace is—the miracle of His mysterious workings in our lives and His exceeding love for us. Susan's story made me "re-joice" in the joy of what salvation really means.

—THETUS TENNEY
COAUTHOR, HOW TO CHASE GOD WHILE CHASING KIDS

This book is a collaborative work with Pat King. Thank you, Pat, for helping me tell my story. Pat King is the international author of eighteen books and Bible studies. She lives in Des Moines, Washington, with her husband, Bill. They have ten children and nineteen grandchildren.

One
Touch

One Touch

SUSAN LANA HAFNER

WITH PAT KING

CREATION
HOUSE
A STRANG COMPANY

ONE TOUCH by Susan Hafner with Pat King
Published by Creation House
A Strang Company
600 Rinehart Road
Lake Mary, Florida 32746
www.strangbookgroup.com

Author's note: This is a true story, but in an effort to not hurt anyone by the writing of this book, some of the people's names have been changed.

Design Director: Bill Johnson

Cover design by Amanda Potter

Library of Congress Control Number: 2009935579
International Standard Book Number: 978-1-59979-948-3

First Edition

09 10 11 12 13 — 987654321
Printed in the United States of America

This book is dedicated to all of you who are sleeping or who will sleep on a One Touch Snuggle Pillow, One Touch Pillowcase, or under a One Touch mosquito net. Our worldwide prayer network is praying for you night after night that God will awaken your heart.

CHAPTER
ONE

I WAS TWELVE WHEN MAMA and I packed everything up and went to my aunt's in Louisiana, where Mama was born and raised. We moved into one of the rooms in the bar that my aunt and her husband, Bob, owned. It had no windows; really, it was an old storeroom. Mama worked as a barmaid.

One weeknight a bunch of the patrons went with Mama and me to my aunt's house. After a couple of hours of drinking, my aunt's husband began raging about someone stealing money from him. He threw a punch at my aunt and hit her squarely in the face. He threw another punch at Mama's boyfriend-for-the-night. Mama tried to calm him down. She put her hand on his chest as she said, "Bob, come on. Stop that now." He knocked her across the room.

I pulled Mama to her feet, grabbed my aunt by the arm, and dragged them both outside, where I thought it was safe. Bob ran after us and started hitting my aunt with his fist. He slammed her to the ground and shouted, "Where's my money?" He kicked her in the head. Her arms, face, and ears bled into the dirt.

I hit him, saying, "Stop it." He knocked me to the ground, too.

I thought he was going to kill her. I got up and ran into the back of the house and yelled to him, "Bob, come look in the house." I was trying to distract him. My aunt was left abandoned in the yard. I ran back outside and helped her crawl into the woods to hide. I raced as fast as I could the three blocks down the country road to the closest neighbor. Trembling so much I could hardly talk, I managed to blurt out, "My aunt was in a fight with her husband. She needs an ambulance." They helped me call the sheriff instead.

1

I ran back to the woods and checked on my aunt first. She was either passed out from alcohol or knocked out from the repeated blows to her head. I could hear the loud country music coming from the house playing on the record player. Hank Williams was singing "I'm So Lonesome I Could Cry." I ran to check on Mama next. She was kissing on her boyfriend. No one seemed to be upset over what had just happened.

Mama greeted the deputy sheriff at the screen door when he arrived. She was no stranger to this role. The authorities had come to our house or bar many times throughout the years to break up drunken brawls, question Mama about shoplifting, or investigate shots fired. That night her own sister had been beaten up. The man who had beaten her was hiding in the back room, still filled with rage and ready to pounce on anyone the moment the deputy left.

Mama responded to the deputy's inquiries by flirting with him. She put her hand on his arm and drawled out, "Oh, my sister and her husband just had a little argument. Everyone's fine. I'm so sorry you had to come way out here." The deputy in his crisp tan uniform flirted back with Mama for a few minutes. He left. The rest of the guests left. Even Bob left. No one asked about my aunt. Mama and I found my aunt in the woods and took her to the emergency room. She had a concussion and four fractures in her face. Her eardrum had been damaged.

Nothing made sense to me. Sitting in the emergency room, I felt like I was in the twilight zone. Then I saw a small pool of blood on the floor. I had become so caught up in taking care of everyone else that I had not even noticed the large bleeding gash on the back of my leg.

But that was my life with Mama.

The earliest memory I have is at three and one-half years old when Mama and Daddy got divorced. We were living in Miami, Florida. After the divorce, when I was four, I had to go live with someone called "Nanny." I guess Mama couldn't take care of me. I spent every day wishing I could be with her. The house where I stayed had a big living room and a long hallway of bedrooms. I remember it looked like a motel.

Mama said this stranger, Nanny, would be my foster mother. I didn't understand.

The kids made fun of me at the dinner table because I didn't want the food. Many times I had to sit alone at the table because I hadn't eaten all my dinner. One night the plate in front of me had on it stewed tomatoes that I refused to eat. I didn't refuse with my words. I wasn't rebellious. I was scared to eat them.

Nanny came in, saw me sitting there, and gave me no choice. She grabbed a spoon and forced the stewed tomatoes into my mouth. I gagged, choked, and threw up on my plate! Then she was really mad. She grabbed me around my waist and hauled me to the kitchen sink. She washed my mouth out with sudsy dishwater.

Mama came and got me three months later and brought me home to a pretty white house in Miami. After being at Nanny's I never wanted to be separated from Mama again. She signed me up for kindergarten, and each day I rode home in the kindergarten station wagon. I could hardly wait to be back with her.

Mama was thirty-one and beautiful, and she knew it. She always looked like she had just stepped out of a magazine. Her dark brown wavy hair shone. She had big brown eyes and a smile that I adored. She had a perfect round face, perfect lips, perfect nose—she seemed perfect all over.

I remember how I raced up our front steps one day when the station wagon stopped. I hoped so much that she was alone because usually Mama had her boyfriend, Tom, come to visit. I opened the door and looked around. He was there. He and Mama stood in the kitchen, each with a bottle of beer in their hands.

Mama didn't seem to realize I was home. She kept talking and laughing with Tom, so I walked quietly into the kitchen, stood beside her, and didn't say anything. After a while I got tired of waiting for her to notice me. I left the kitchen, went into the living room, and sat on the edge of the brown sofa. I listened to them laughing. I wished I could be part of that laughter, but it was special for Tom.

If she wasn't home when the station wagon dropped me off, I had to sit and wait for her to come in, sometimes for a long time. So, having her home in the kitchen with Tom was a lot better than not having her home at all.

I had curly cotton-white hair. Like Mama, I had a dark tan from the Miami sun. My face wasn't as full of life as hers. I was thin and serious looking.

I never thought much of eating anything after school because Mama never left me anything to eat. In my young life I had learned not to enjoy food. It had become a necessity, not a pleasure. There was no way I could have known then that Mama had an obsessive compulsive disorder that revolved around food and drink. She had so much fear and anxiety whenever she ate; I'm sure that's why I had an aversion to food.

I have a picture of Mama and Daddy in his uniform. They are in a bar, and my dad is holding a drink. I can't see his blue eyes because they are closed. He had the same olive complexion as me. He was easily recognized as a Finn: low forehead, prominent cheekbones, round face. Both of my grandparents came from Finland. I wish I could have met them, but I didn't. I definitely inherited the trait common to the Finns, *sisu*, which means "persistent determination"!

I was named after my dad's mother and my dad, Arne. "Susan Arnene Pete" is what is on my birth certificate. I was "Susan" for three years. After they divorced, Mama started calling me another name, Lana. She liked the Lana Turner, Hollywood movie star, glitzy image. I think she saw herself as part of the jet set.

Then Mama met Hank. He was twenty years older than she, and he was an alcoholic. She worked for him in his bar. They both had a drink in their hands whenever I saw them.

One morning Mama said, "Lana, Hank and I have good news." She sat beside me all pretty and sparkly.

I held my breath. What could it be? Something good, surely.

She kept smiling, "We've found a boarding school for you. You will live there."

I don't remember how I responded to such terrible news. Did I cry or protest? Probably not. I couldn't fight Mama. But in my heart I know I cried. I was going to be away from her again.

They sent me to the Cuban-owned Nance's Boarding School. It was like a prison to me. The school was completely fenced in. I thought I'd done something wrong for them to lock me up at this school. I promised myself, "I will study real hard and do everything Mama and Hank want me to do so I can get out of here."

I hated nights. They were lonely. I had a center room with no windows. My room had one dim light, so it was always shadowy and scary. When I woke up I never knew if it was day or night. I found it difficult to understand any of the adults. They spoke Spanish to each other and very broken English to us who were not Cuban.

I could only tell when it was morning by the sounds. As soon as I heard the other kids, I threw on my shorts, shirt, and sandals and rushed to the classroom. All of our classes were in a big, long room with ceiling-to-floor louvered glass windows on both sides. The kitchen was in an adjoining room, and every morning I hoped no one would notice that I wasn't at the breakfast table. I still did not like to eat.

I did all of my first grade work and spent the rest of the time longing for Mama. I learned to converse in Spanish a little. My picture appeared in a Cuban newspaper. I was the youngest to complete a *caneva* at Nance's. I had embroidered numerous art pieces. I made two sets of pillowcases for my mama with "To mother with love" and flowers around it. Later on I never saw any of the pieces I had made for Mama at our house.

I kept thinking, *If I do good enough, Mama and Hank will come and take me away from here.* I asked my teacher, "Can I put my papers on the wall? I want my mama to see how good I'm doing." I begged her not to take them down, but Mama never did go to the classroom.

I was frequently left alone in the large lunchroom. My teacher said in her broken English, "Lana, you stay. You finish you supper." One night I sat by myself even after it became dark. No one was around, so I felt my way to the trashcan, scraped the food off my plate, and went to bed.

I was so happy on the days Mama came and picked me up for a weekend. We went to her one-room apartment. We never ate together because Mama had to eat separately from everybody. She spent lots of time at the sink washing things. She explained, "I have to wash the poison off." We sat in bed together and read the funny papers. We laughed together at the antics of Dagwood and Blondie. I loved that! The time with her was always too short. I could stay there forever.

The first remembrance I have of my being sick was while I was at Nance's. I had a cold. Mama came to pick me up for a weekend. I was so excited. I watched for her through the louvered windows. I ran and hugged her as she came to the classroom door. "Mama!"

Immediately she backed away from me. "Are you sick?"

I beamed at her. "No, Mama."

My teacher explained, "Oh, she just has a little cold."

Mama had rheumatic fever as a child, and it left her with a heart murmur. She began a narrative that I would hear many, many more times throughout my life: "The doctor told me I have to stay healthy because of my heart murmur. I can't be around anyone who is sick." Although this was grossly exaggerated in her mind, it was real to her.

She gave me a strained hug. "Goodbye, Lana. I can't be near you when you're sick." She smiled at me. I smiled back—but only with my lips. She turned and walked away. I watched her through the windows for much longer than she could be seen. I could see her in my heart even though I couldn't see her with my eyes. It was my fault. I was sick, and that could cause *her* to die. The longer I blankly stared out the window, the more lost I felt. I wanted to run after her crying, screaming, "Please, please don't leave me!" I wanted to grab her and not let go. But I didn't. I couldn't. I had no voice. I sobbed inwardly, my emotions tucked deep inside. Sadness shrouded me like a cloak. I wrapped myself in it and walked away from the window.

CHAPTER
TWO

FINALLY, IT WAS THE last day of first grade. Mama and Hank came and picked me up. She told me that she and Hank had gotten married. We drove straight to a big, gray house. I thought, *This must be where my mama and Hank live, and now me too!* We walked up the sidewalk. Hank rang the doorbell. When a lady answered the door, Mama said, "This is Jenny. Lana, you are going to stay with her." We walked inside. Before I could even understand what was happening, Mama left.

I started crying, "Why didn't she even tell me good-bye?"

I don't remember what Jenny looked like, what the house looked like, what we did. All I remember is Mama left, and I didn't know if she would ever come back.

She did come back, three months later. I stayed close beside her walking down the stairs. Mama, at last. She was always so pretty and full of smiles, and her eyes looked so beautiful to me. Her words broke my heart. "Lana, I'm taking you to Nance's to start second grade."

No, no, no, Mama. Please, no, I thought. I asked her, "Am I going to have to stay there?"

Mama didn't answer me. She left me again.

A month later, Mama came and moved me out. At last we could be together. As soon as we got to the car, she announced, "You are going to go live in Hammond, Louisiana." I couldn't even understand what her words meant.

At the age of seven I flew to New Orleans—alone. I was going to live with my mother's older sister, Aunt Daisy, and her husband, Doc. They had four children. The twins, Nancy and Carl, were a year older than I was. Apparently Aunt Daisy had told Mama, "I feel sorry for Lana living at that school. Let her come live with us, and I can have triplets."

It was late at night when Bobby, Aunt Daisy's older son, and his new wife, Janice, picked me up at the airport. By now I was used to strange new situations. I had learned it did no good to protest; just go with it. But inside I was scared. I was always scared. Bobby and Janice put me to bed in a room with cousins who were strangers. I felt alone, like I was dangling in midair.

The first day at my new school I took tests all day. I must have done well because my teacher said, "You're going to skip second grade and go into third. You'll be able to be in the same classroom with your twin cousins."

Aunt Daisy's family, the Hyde family, was well known in the Hammond area. Uncle Doc owned Hyde's Slaughterhouse and Meat Packing. The twins were well liked and leaders in just about everything at school. Everyone wanted to be around them. I awkwardly stayed in the background.

My cousin, Nancy, was beautiful. She had dark brown hair, dark eyes, and a dark complexion. She was sweet and prissy and self-assured in a good way. Carl had a buzz cut and freckles. I was a mousy intruder scared of both of them. Still, I tagged along, proud to be their cousin.

This was the first time I had ever been with relatives. It was also the first time I experienced what I call normal family life. We ate three meals at a table together. Aunt Daisy wasn't afraid of being poisoned. She wasn't afraid I might kill her if I got sick. Actually, she mothered me and took care of me when I was sick. The family made fudge two or three times a month regularly. *Regularly*—that was a word I didn't use often before I lived with them. My regularly had been, "I can regularly depend on nothing."

Aunt Daisy looked like my mother, except without all the glitter and pretense. She had soft skin, and she smelled of sweet bath powder. She did motherly things for me. She helped me get dressed for school, she took me to the doctor and dentist, and she cooked for us. I learned to enjoy hearing her say, "Breakfast is ready." Aunt

Daisy sewed for me and the twins. We often had matching outfits. I liked that very much. I belonged in this family unit. Or at least it looked like I belonged. I was amazed to find out that this is what family is all about. I loved Aunt Daisy and Uncle Doc. I began to call them Mom and Dad. It felt natural.

I learned to do something living at Aunt Daisy's that I'd never done before. I learned to compare. When I compared myself to the others I always felt second rate to everyone, except Aunt Daisy.

I remember my first Christmas there. We got up early in the morning. Nancy said, "Look at all the presents under the tree!" Of course there was a gang of us: Aunt Daisy and Uncle Doc; Bobby and Janice; JoAnn, the older sister; the twins; and me. I liked it that Bobby and Janice were there. They were the ones who had met me at the airport, so I felt a special connection with them. I loved them, and thought they liked me. This particular Christmas, I watched to see what they had gotten the twins.

The item wasn't important—what mattered was that my gift from them would equal what they got the twins. If mine was less, it said they thought I was second rate and I didn't deserve something as good as "family" members. That really was the only present I was focused on. I quietly, slowly opened my gift from them, hoping, hoping it was something as good as the twins had gotten. I had been left out so much, I braced myself for that pain.

They gave me a purse, a pretty little purse. It was much better than Nancy and Carl's gift. I thought it was the nicest gift under the tree. I was special to Bobby and Janice! They liked me! That Christmas lasted me a very long time. I felt so happy that I mattered to them.

The next Christmas, the twins each got stunning blue bikes. After the twins got their bikes, one of them said sassily to me, "We got bikes and you didn't." I was paralyzed. I didn't know how to respond. By then I believed for sure that I was inferior.

After the sassy remark, Aunt Daisy rolled my bike out! It was lighter blue, a little smaller—because I was smaller—and it had training wheels and a bell on it! I loved it! I loved it! Aunt Daisy knew I would be surprised. I was pretty much surprised anytime someone was extra nice to me.

The twins learned to ride right away, and I couldn't ride without the training wheels. Of course, we all couldn't ride together, so they would go off and leave me. My older cousin, Pete, came to visit us a few months after Christmas. He took time with me and taught me how to ride. We would go up and down the dirt road between the house and the slaughterhouse. He patiently persisted, and I learned in one day. I loved Pete for taking time to help me.

As much as I liked watching this family unit in action, there was a major glitch. I realized quickly the twins were not as receptive to my being there as Aunt Daisy was. They were used to being the cute twins, but now they were forced to share that attention with me, especially when Aunt Daisy said, "These are the triplets." I didn't have their social skills or their popularity. I felt like a dud tagging along with them. When they were invited to parties that I was not asked to, they thought it was very funny that I didn't get to go.

Sometimes it was even worse when Aunt Daisy made me go with them! Then, for sure, I was an outsider interfering in their lives. I would sit in the corner in complete horror. I felt uninvited, unknown, and unwanted. I felt ugly and unsure of myself. All I wanted was to blend into the wall. I didn't just feel uncomfortable; in my mind I was a fish out of water. Nancy and Carl laughed and talked to the other children who crowded around them. As I watched them interact, all I could do was stare blankly. I couldn't copy their actions because I didn't understand them. In my world, no one wanted to laugh with me. No one wanted to crowd around and listen to me. I had no clue how to interact. I felt lost and alone, unable to relate to their happy chatter.

There was always activity at Aunt Daisy's. Most of the time the twins sided with each other and left me out. Standing on the sidelines, I told myself, "You don't belong." Here I was finally a member of a family, and I felt I wasn't wanted. I didn't fit. It was one of the most wounding times of my childhood, feeling I wasn't loved. However, I did feel Aunt Daisy tried to help me.

I hadn't seen Mama for almost a year when one morning Aunt Daisy came to the breakfast table with a big smile. "Guess who was on the phone? Lana, it was your Mama. She's coming to visit." Oh, wow! My heart raced with happiness. This was going to be great. Everyone was excited that she was coming. She and Hank had divorced since I'd been gone, and I had worried about her. Now I would get to see her and hug her and sit beside her.

She surprised us all. She brought Hank with her. The whole household was giddy over her arrival. She was the "movie star" aunt and sister who blew in from Miami. She had that air about her that dominated a room. She was glamorous and loved the attention. I loved giving it to her, but she hardly noticed me. Her visit was taken over by her surprise announcement: "Hank and I are going down to the Covington courthouse to get married again!" They did. The next day they left. Mama had come and gone, and I hardly spent any time with her at all.

Then, Uncle Doc had a stroke, and Aunt Daisy could no longer take care of me. Even though I missed Mama, the longing for a normal family was so strong that I didn't want to leave when I was sent back to Miami. I was going to miss the routine. I was going to miss the smell of fresh sausage from the slaughterhouse and fresh cane syrup, the consistency of three meals a day and all eating together. The family unit, happiness, enjoying food for the first time, even the squabbles were endearing to me. They seemed like normal family times.

Even though I didn't feel like I belonged there, even though I didn't feel like I fit in, I didn't want to be sent away. Living there was like watching a TV program. In my mind, I knew I wasn't a part of the story, but I was totally absorbed in the fairy tale I was watching. Aunt Daisy was my mother substitute. Inside I cried out, *Don't send me away.*

Family life was over. Three meals a day were over. Stability was over. I was nine years old.

CHAPTER
THREE

MY FIRST NIGHT BACK in Miami, we went to Chuck's house. He was one of Hank and Mama's friends. Mama introduced me to a roomful of people: "This is my daughter, who God gave me to take care of me." They all held up their glasses and cheered me. We stayed late that night. I sat next to Mama and watched them laugh and drink.

My life became clearer. I understood now that life was not about me. It was about Mama. I told myself that I didn't need anything. My life with Aunt Daisy had been wonderful. I had a chance at being mothered, but that was not where I fit or belonged.

Late that night we climbed the stairs to my new home. Our living quarters were above a bar with a short-order restaurant and package liquor store. It would be my home off and on for almost four years. It was not homey. There were no decorations. The bedrooms were big and cold. I had my own room across from Mama and Hank's. During the day and especially late into the night I could hear the barroom noises: the jukebox loudly playing, the pinball machine, the people at the bar laughing and talking.

I knew about bars; I had been in them with Mama before I went to boarding school. When Mama first worked for Hank, he was still married to someone else. She took me there often. It wasn't long before she began to call Hank her boyfriend. Mama flirted with most men. She would laughingly tell me, "Any man would be glad to be my boyfriend, even if he's married." I guess Hank was one of those men.

My new life at the bar was a huge contrast to living at the farm with my Louisiana relatives. Here in Miami, barroom fights were normal. I hated the yelling. I hated the anger. I hated the fistfights. I hated the police coming.

Mama was consumed by the barroom activity, consumed by her fear of being poisoned, consumed by her alcoholism, and consumed with men. There was a huge difference in the way she treated me and the way Aunt Daisy had treated me. But somehow I understood Mama wasn't able to take care of me the way her sister had. Now it was my job to take care of her, like Aunt Daisy had taken care of me. Deep down I knew that I must not let Mama feel any responsibility for me. If I were a burden to her I would be sent away. I must not need anything. I must be as obedient as I could be.

I matured fast that first year back from Louisiana. Even though I was nine, I broke up fights between her and Hank. One night after we closed the bar, I heard Mama and Hank fighting in the storeroom. Hank accused Mama, "I saw you kissing him! Don't tell me you aren't seeing him!"

I ran in to see Hank swinging his big arms toward Mama. They were both drunk. Mama's face was already bleeding. I yelled, "Stop it. Stop it." I beat on his stomach. Hank stood six feet tall and weighed over 250 pounds. He was not deterred by my attempt to defend my mama. But he was distracted, and that gave her time to run out of the room and into the dark.

I chased him and yelled, "Leave her alone!"

He never acknowledged I was there. Although that night Mama did not call the police, there were many nights that she did.

Despite the fighting, I liked Hank. He was a distinguished, well-known businessman. He had white or grayish wavy hair. He had a full, round red face and puffy eyes, probably because of the alcoholism. I don't really know why I liked him, except that he did want to take care of my mama. He fought with her because he was jealous of her. Even though life was chaotic, Mama and I had a place to live together.

I got up each morning before they did and walked downstairs. Before I opened the door leading to the lounge, I had to turn off the burglar alarm. I stood on my tiptoes and used a broom handle

to reach up and trip the alarm so it wouldn't go off. My job was to
refill the beer boxes behind the bar counter and restock the package
liquor store. My reward was the change I found under the barstools.
I could generally judge if I was going to collect a few coins or many
by the noise the night before.

As I lay in bed trying to go to sleep, I became pretty good at eval-
uating the crowd below. The noisier they were, the drunker they
were. The drunker they were, the more they fumbled with their
money and dropped it on the floor. That drunken crowd would also
wind up leaving coins in the "return change" spaces in the jukebox
and pinball and cigarette machines.

Hank often asked me how much money I'd found. I'd proudly
declare my findings. He would then challenge me to play gin rummy
with him. I always lost my money to him. He would laugh good-
naturedly. Weird. I thought grownups generally let little kids
win—at least sometimes!

Mama's boyfriends were a source of drama. At some point, Mama
and Hank wanted to have a little break to work on their marriage.
Mama and I moved out of the bar into a duplex about a block away.
One night Hank came over to the duplex drunk. Of course, that was
usual for both of them. I was sitting on the floor in my shorts and
pajama top playing Monopoly alone. Hank came in yelling, "Where's
your mama?"

"She's at the neighbors; I'll get her." I jumped up and ran out the
back door before he could say anything else. I went to the other
apartment and knocked on the bedroom window whispering, yet
hollering, "Hank is here!" That had been one of many times Mama
had sneaked away to "visit" Earl. He was a detective, which intrigued
her. It seemed like a glamorous career to Mama. He even had a
flashing red light on his dashboard. When Mama came running in
the door, all breathless, Hank begged her to come back.

Besides her boyfriends, Hank argued with Mama about the way
she washed everything because of her fear of being poisoned. "I'm
not going to kill you! Quit washing that stuff!"

Mama stood up to him, "I have to. It's me they're poisoning, not
you."

I didn't understand why she was afraid of everyone, even me! She bought her liquor in miniatures by the case and hid the cases under the bed. She wouldn't order them through our package liquor store but went to another store. Actually, she kept changing liquor stores.

Mama drank all day. Each time she made a drink, she retrieved one miniature bottle of Cutty Sark Scotch. Then she went to a light and rotated that bottle over and over and over again examining the seal, looking to see if it had been tampered with. Mama's fear of people poisoning her occupied so much of her thinking that she imagined things were happening that weren't.

One time I thought I would help her make her drink. I reached under the bed and pulled out the case of miniature bottles of Scotch. She went into a rage! "Why are you doing that? Give me that! What do you have in your pockets?" She angrily turned my empty pockets inside out and then grabbed the whole box and fled out the door. She threw the whole case away and bought a new one.

That was the last day I ever interfered in Mama's obsessive-compulsive rituals. It hurt me that she thought I would harm her. Why had she screamed at me? Why had she left? The pain of her rejection made me feel like my heart had no home. My heart had been tagging along behind my mama, wanting her approval, her love, her acceptance, her comfort, her care—her trust. I stood in the living room alone that day and told myself what I had come to believe: *I am not important in life except for one reason, to take care of Mama. What I feel does not matter.*

Mama taught me to drink at age nine. I was with her in a package liquor store in south Miami when she said, "I am going to buy us each a bottle of wine." I never questioned anything. She bought a fifth of Harvey's Amontillado and a fifth of Harvey's Bristol Cream. She let me try a shot glass of each. "Which do you like best?" Actually, it all tasted the same to me, but I was certainly not going to tell her that. She had brought me into her adult world, and I wasn't going to let her down. I confidently blurted out, "The Bristol Cream." So now we had something new to share. I was thrilled for any bonding opportunity with her. I felt it was me and Mama against the world. I would protect her, be her confidant, take care of her, and now drink with her!

When I went down to clean the bar in the mornings, I made myself a drink of some sort of sherry or a sweet grenadine drink. Mama giggled when I told her what I did. At night I sometimes worked as bartender. I knew how to make all the fancy drinks. I had to stand on my tiptoes to put drinks on the bar. I was a child only in age. I lived in an adult world and was not expected to act like a child.

Despite everything I was doing for Mama, she sent me away again. I really don't know why. I lived with someone named Dormus on Miami Beach, but all I wanted was to be back at the bar with Mama. I was so shy I hardly talked at all. I had to stay three months.

Another time Mama made me go live with someone named Merle. "Please, Mama. You need me. Don't send me away!" Mama had no answers or direction for her own life, and she certainly didn't for me. It was futile for me to speak up about anything. Life revolved around her, not me. Merle had her own children, and I felt humiliated when she introduced me as the foster child. Finally, I was able to move back with Mama.

There were so many men in and out of our lives I couldn't keep track of them. Hank raged about it. I had to change schools whenever Mama ran off with another man. Once we left Hank and moved in with Mama's boyfriend, Bill, and his sister. They had a big, luxurious home with a pool. Mama usually went for men with money or prestige.

I slept in the same bed as Mama and Bill. They ignored me when they had sex. The first time it happened, I was terrified and confused. What was going on? I curled up in a ball and went somewhere else in my head. What I wanted didn't matter. I was a non-person, not allowed to speak up for what I wanted. I didn't want to be there with Mama and Bill that night, but even greater than my confusion was my perpetual fear of being sent away again. After a few months with Bill, I was relieved when we moved back to the bar and I could sleep in my own bed alone.

Sometimes Mama and I sneaked off to go see Jim Turner. He was a pilot and had a big house. Mama kept telling me she wanted to marry him so I would be Lana Turner and have the same name as the Hollywood actress. Mama really tried to pull me into her fantasy world.

We had quiet drinking parties at Jim's. He seemed like a distinguished man. Mama would bring "our" wine. She had changed my brand and proudly and unashamedly told Jim, "Lana's favorite is Liebfraumilch." I guess it sounded more stylish. I think Mama liked for me to drink because her drinking didn't stand out as much.

No one ever appeared to frown on my drinking. One man said, "Oh, how cute."

I became a novelty to Mama's boyfriends, a part of the drinking party. I did what I was told. "Sit on Jim's lap." "Dance with Bill." "Give Earl a big hug." I didn't like that. They were Mama's boyfriends, not mine. No one seemed to realize that I was just a child. Some of them acted like they were my boyfriends, too. They kissed on me and put their hands all over me like they did Mama.

I did what I had to do to survive and cope. In the midst of the stress, confusion, and hurt, I would blank out. It was like my brain literally went numb. I could not leave physically, so I left emotionally. When I was trapped in the continual sexual abuse and neglect, I went to my I-don't-belong world and shifted into self-talk: *It does not matter what happens to me. I am a non-person.* It comforted me to believe that I was a non-person. That meant that I didn't have to experience the feelings of the extreme anguish and trauma of the moment. In my head I went far away, sometimes into a black hole.

I continued to be quiet, unobtrusive, polite, and helpful in serving drinks. Mama started wanting me around more and more. I needed her to need me so I could be with her. She *finally* began to bond with me, "the little girl that God gave me to take care of me." We both knew that was my purpose in life. That was what cemented our relationship. That was what kept us together. She began to call me her "pumpkin." Secretly I liked that! I didn't know where she ended and I began. There was no need to speak up for things I liked, disliked, or didn't understand. I did whatever Mama wanted.

Later, when I read about an animal chewing off its leg to get out of a trap in order to survive, I knew this was what I had done. My life had been about survival; better to go on living with only three legs than to die with all four. By chewing off an emotional part of me, I was able to live with what I had no power to change. I really don't know what to name it or call it, but I lived through the trauma by separating from a significant part of who I was.

Out of all Mama's boyfriends, Hank was her favorite. She married him three times. Even though she and Hank fought constantly, she was attached to him. He was her father-figure who wanted to take care of her. Yet, they fought all the time.

I remember once when Mama and I left Hank and moved in with Don. I changed schools again. I got off the bus on a hot, sunny Miami day and walked the block to the apartment Mama, Don, and I were living in. When I got to the front door, I saw glass everywhere. The windows in the door had been broken. As I peered in, I saw Hank sitting on the couch. His hand was bleeding profusely. He was drunk. I knew my role well. Bandage Hank's hand. Comfort him. Ignore the situation. Make small talk so we didn't have to have a major confrontation. Protect Mama.

Hank demanded to know, "Where's your mother? Is she with Don?"

I didn't know where Mama was. All I knew is I didn't want her to walk in right then, but she did. I expected a fistfight. Hank grabbed Mama, hugged her, and began crying. We quickly packed up and moved back to the bar in Miami.

The morning I found a cigarette lighter discarded in a trashcan was the day I became an entrepreneur. I took it out of the trash and added lighter fluid. It worked great and looked new. I decided to use it to make some money. I put beans in a jar. For twenty-five cents people at the bar could guess how many beans were in the jar, and whoever was closest could win the lighter. I walked around with a notepad for about a week and got the bar patrons to buy a chance.

Hank got a jar the same size and filled it with beans. He counted them and then gave me twenty-five cents and his estimate. He won. I never understood why he was always trying to outsmart me.

I picked kumquats from a tree in a vacant lot next to the bar. I set up a basket by the cash register in the package liquor store with a sign, "Kumquats for sale. Two for a penny." I asked Hank to buy me a carton of eggs at the grocer. I paid him twenty-five cents for the eggs and boiled them. I set up a second basket at the bar counter with a sign in the basket that read, "Hard boiled eggs for sale ten cents each."

I watched Hank pay bills in his office and asked him financial questions. "How much do you pay for a case of beer? Do all the brands cost the same?" Then I figured out how much profit he and Mama made on each bottle of beer. I was fascinated by business. I liked filling the beer boxes and counting how many had been sold the night before. I could figure out how much money Mama and Hank made on the sale of the beer.

When I was eleven, Mama decided to run away from Hank again. We moved to Key West to a motel. Mama went to work at a night-club, and I stayed home alone and waited.

I remember a time when I was really hungry and Mama came home from the nightclub with no food. When she woke up the next day, she went straight to work. I guess she forgot about me not eating. By nighttime, I figured it was up to me to be resourceful. I broke a vodka bottle bank, took the little bit of change and walked in the dark to the corner grocery. I bought a moon pie to eat. I hadn't eaten since the day before at lunch.

When Mama came home that night and saw the broken bottle, she was furious. "How dare you break my bottle and steal the money!" She walked out the door and left me standing there humiliated and alone. Her rejection made me feel like my heart had no home. I wanted her love, approval, and acceptance so much. It was like the time when she had left me in the big gray house and walked out. Once more, I stood alone in the middle of a living room, feeling hopeless and without help. An abandoned child.

Life was completely about Mama and the trials and tribulations of *her* life. Once more I told myself, *I'm not important in life except to take care of Mama. I don't matter. I am nothing.*

CHAPTER
FOUR

WE MOVED TO LOUISIANA and moved in with Mama's new boyfriend, Henry. She assumed his last name. I slept in the bed next to her and Henry. I hated it. My escape was to go somewhere else in my head. I told myself, *Don't look for an escape; there is none. This crazy world with my mama is the only place I fit in.*

At age thirty-eight, Mama's appearance was not as neat and kept. She wore way too much makeup, gaudy jewelry, and always chose the latest movie star trends. She sprayed her hair with pink and silver highlights. She wore go-go boots. I hated the look. I wanted a wholesome mother who smelled of sweet powder and freshly baked cookies. Mama often said to me, "Pumpkin, can't you add a little color to your face? You can always wear some of my jewelry. You look so plain." I knew I was plain. I loved Mama, but I didn't want to look like her.

Henry worked out of town sometimes, and Mama entertained other men in his house when he wasn't there. She met these men at clubs. I usually sat outside in the car while Mama stayed in the bars for hours. I often met Mama's boyfriend-for-the-night when he came out to the car to "check on me." Over and over I coped the only way I knew how. If they violated me, I told myself, "I'm a nobody, a non-person. I don't matter."

A man named Mil began to come over regularly to "visit" while Henry was at work. One night he and Mama wanted to drive ten miles to a nightclub. Mil handed me the keys and said, "Hey, Lana, you drive us." I had never driven before. Mil gave me a few instructions, and we took off.

On the hood of Mil's red-and-white Buick there was a large airplane-looking hood ornament. I found out that if I lined up the nose of that ornament with the stripe on the right side of the road, then I could keep the car in our lane. That was it! I was the designated driver from then on. It would be three years more before I was eligible to get a driver's permit. That seemed totally irrelevant to everyone.

Mil was in our lives for about two months when Mama asked me, "What would you think if we all went to the Covington courthouse and Mil and I got married?" It was comical how I generally was always included in the dialog of decision-making, but my choices never mattered. We moved out of Henry's house, and Mama and Mil got married that day.

After they got married, word got back to us that Mama's last boyfriend, Henry, was trying to find her to kill her. Of course, Mama thought Henry was the one who was crazy!

Mil worked out of town, and when he came home he did nothing but stretch out on the couch with his feet propped up on the back, drink beer, smoke cigars, and watch TV. When he wasn't around, Mama called him her fat boyfriend. But I was glad they got married so there would be someone to take care of Mama. Their bedroom was directly across the hall from mine. They usually left their door open. The fact that I could hear and see everything that went on in their bedroom did not bother them. I turned the radio on to drown them out.

I didn't cook. Mama was the one who hovered around the kitchen area. She didn't want me or anyone around when she cooked. She sent me to the store to buy the food and whatever condiments we would eat for the day. Every day she ordered, "Now, Pumpkin, make sure the items are clean and no one has tried to get into them."

At home she scrutinized the items to make sure no one had added any poison to them. If the groceries I bought passed her inspection, she put a date and time on each item. If something didn't pass her inspection, I had to go back to the store with some lame excuse to exchange it. The next day we followed the same routine. After using the food items they were stored in the cabinets and refrigerator, never to be used again. Only she knew why she didn't discard them. One night Mama and Mil argued about this weird behavior. He began pulling food out of the refrigerator and cabinets, saying, "I'm living with a crazy woman! There is a date and time on *everything* we eat." He lined up the various food items in groups and counted them. "Here are fourteen jars of mayonnaise. Fifteen packages of butter. Twelve loaves of bread. Fifteen boxes of salt." The list went on.

Mama's Scotch bottles each had a date and time on them as well. Mil had great fun harassing Mama about this. In the middle of one of their fistfights, the neighbors called the police. Mil began ranting to the cops, "This woman is insane! She doesn't even drink all the Scotch out of the bottles." He ran into my bedroom with the policemen following and lifted up my mattress. "See all these bottles!" He pulled them out from under my mattress and lined them up on the floor.

"Look, she even hides them in her daughter's dresser!" He rummaged through my clothes, pulling out more bottles. He counted his find. "Thirty-eight bottles! Look! She leaves at least two inches of Scotch in the bottom of every bottle because she thinks if it is poisoned, the poison will sink to the bottom. Nuts! Nuts! I am telling you she is nuts!" He continued to shout, "She never throws the bottles away. She never throws the food away."

I stood between Mama and my stepfather's outburst. This was a normal day. If it wasn't this drama, it was something else.

Often Mama's sisters came to the house and collected all the barely touched food and liquor and took it to their homes. It was quite a bonanza for them. Other times Mama and I gathered everything up and took it to a poor area across town and gave it all away.

We never ate at a dining table. We ate on TV trays. I got up one time during a meal to answer the phone. Before I could get to the phone, she stopped me. She thought I'd thrown poison in her food. "Here, taste my food." She pushed it in my mouth. "Here, try this." She shoved something else from her plate in my mouth. After that I seldom made the mistake of leaving my TV tray. Mama's rule was:

don't get near my food or drink. I was too young to understand that this kind of behavior was a form of mental illness.

I think Mama loved me as much as she could. But, she saw me as another part of herself. She didn't seem to realize that I had thoughts and feelings of my own. Every independent idea I had she squashed, as if it was not one bit important.

I really had a hard time knowing what it was I wanted for myself. I saw the neighborhood kids riding around on their bikes. I had a fleeting thought that it would be nice if I had one. I couldn't allow myself to form the words *I want*, even in my mind. My life revolved around Mama's choices. "Hey, Pumpkin, why don't you and I go to The Continental tonight? They have a new band playing." I didn't like her choices, but that was just how it was. Her addictions and obsessions took all of her thoughts and energy. I never challenged her. For her to ignore what I wanted was normal. It was all I had ever known!

At age thirteen, we moved to Denham Springs, Louisiana, where Mil was from. I began my freshman year at Denham Springs High School, where I would later graduate. This was a big change, settling down for four years at the same school. The permanence of being at the same school, however, brought its own dilemma. As I associated with classmates and teachers at school, I became painfully aware of how different their lives were from mine. I didn't know what to say to these strange people who talked a different language about roller skating or swimming or shopping with friends. I backed further and further into my own world.

Instead, I concentrated on Mama. I became hyper-vigilant in taking care of her. I protected her from criticism and hated for anyone to notice her peculiar behavior. Part of Mama's illness was that she carried around a fifth of Cutty Sark Scotch in a tackle box. She kept a padlock on it, and it was never out of her safekeeping.

In public, while eating in a booth with Mama, she would pull out the tackle box. She also brought her own ice, which was in small pieces from having prewashed it twice before leaving home. If all was quiet, her obvious secretive behavior of making her own drink was more noticeable and brought critical stares from outsiders. As

I saw people at nearby tables watching her, I either engaged them in conversation to distract them from Mama, or I engaged her in conversation so that it appeared we were just average people. We had ordinary bizarre happenings, and then there were the out-of-the-ordinary bizarre events. After being married to Mil for about two years, Mama informed me that she was going to get an attorney so she could file for a divorce from Hank. "Don't tell Mil." She had a smug little smile. Life was a big con game.

When we lived with Mil, we put up a Christmas tree every year. It was a small aluminum tree with red balls. Mama picked it out. It was tinselly and sparkly, like she was, like the ones we had put up in the bar in Miami.

I tried to please Mama with just the right gift; something I thought would be nice for her, like a little silver necklace. Mama could never be happy with what I bought for her, even if I paid a lot of money for it. But what hurt me the most were conversations when she told other people, "Yeah, my daughter got me a fantastic gift," and then made up a lie about some elaborate piece of jewelry. She lived in a grandiose fantasy world that was all her own. It was a world that I tried hard to understand. It was a world that I desperately wanted to be a part of, whether I understood it or not. She was everything to me.

Our Christmases were not about relationships, good cheer, Christmas carols, family, and presents. All the bars closed for Christmas holidays. It was difficult for Mama to deal with the quiet. For her, the exciting holiday was always New Year's Eve. December was about rushing around getting party hats, streamers, noise-makers, confetti, decorations, and balloons for the biggest blowout of the year, New Year's Eve.

I didn't like any kind of celebrations. I didn't like the drinking. I didn't like all her boyfriends. I didn't like the drama. I didn't like the uncertainty. I didn't like the con games. I didn't like the fighting. I didn't like the "crying in your beer" music. And I didn't like New Year's Eve!

CHAPTER

FIVE

I STRUGGLED IN SCHOOL. I wasn't involved in clubs. Mama was still keeping me home often. But my worst downfall was social interaction. I, frankly, did not know how to mingle.

I didn't fit in. I knew I didn't. I knew I couldn't. Sometimes I imitated others, but I didn't know what I was doing. School was a bewildering world. It was like I had the skills of a preschooler trying to participate in high school activities.

When I went through the lunch line, I smiled with my lips at the cafeteria workers who put food on my tray. But the dreaded time always came at the end of the line. *Where would I eat?* No table was better than the other. If a table was filled with lots of kids, I had to endure the "happy talk" conversations. If it was almost empty, I stood out as eating alone.

I remember choosing a table away from the door, against the wall, with three people engaged in conversation. I knew they wouldn't notice me, and I didn't look at them. I began to eat but went somewhere else in my head so I didn't have to listen to them.

Only softly I heard a girl's voice say, "I can't come to your house. My grandma is coming over tonight for a big party. We are going to have a barbeque." They kept talking about family, friends, and what they were going to do. Even to listen faintly was painful. What would have been even worse, though, was for one of them to start talking to me. I wouldn't know what to say. I was an intruder into their normal world. I didn't fit or belong at that table. But I had to sit somewhere.

One day I was sitting at a table when a girl named Dianne excitedly asked a couple of us to attend the revival at Northside Baptist Church. I sort of knew Dianne because we had study hall together. She had big brown eyes and not quite shoulder-length black hair. Almost too afraid to speak out, I said, "Um...um...We just moved by that church. Maybe I can come to the revival."

Well, that was it! I was right in the middle of the conversation. One of the girls said, "That would be great!"

Dianne added, "It will be going on until Sunday night, but come tonight."

Another girl said, "It starts at seven o'clock, but come early."

I was surprised by their reaction. "OK, I'll see you there tonight."

I can't say I had much emotion thinking about going. I had but one motive. This group might be open to including me to eat with them if I attended their church meeting. It would just be one tiny thing that would relieve some awkwardness at school.

Getting away to go on Friday was not easy. By now I was a senior in high school, and still my life didn't revolve around any of my desires. It was still all about Mama. So when Friday night came, Mama had other plans. Mil was working out of town, and Mama decided we would go out of town with a man named J.T. *If I don't go to the revival, I won't be able to sit with Dianne and the other girls at lunch.* But there was no way I could ever explain this to Mama.

Mama's new boyfriend, J. T., presented a scary new twist. He was married. That alone was not unusual. However, he and his wife were parents of a fellow classmate! Once we had gone to J. T.'s house, and I saw pictures of his son. I gasped, *Oh no! I don't want these two worlds to collide!* I feared the normal world condemning us. But Mama and J. T. rode openly around the town where we all lived. It seemed I was the only one trying to be secretive about it.

If I was the one driving, I went down back roads. Mama and J. T. were usually drunk and depending on me, so usually they were oblivious to what I was doing. If it was broad daylight, I suggested we go out of town to eat at a nice restaurant. It would have done no good to mention the fear factor of being seen.

That Friday night I drove us to an out of town bar and motel. We rented one room with two beds. I ignored Mama and J. T. in the other bed, and they ignored me, like I was just another piece of furniture in the room. It was times like these that my heart kept on beating, whether I wanted it to or not.

Mama was not mean. It wasn't that she considered my feelings insignificant. She assumed she knew what I wanted to do. A weekend out of town with an interesting guy, a good bar, loud music, restaurant meals, and a motel room was exactly what she wanted; so it must be what I wanted, too.

Driving home on Sunday I kept thinking about eating lunch the next day and how I'd said I'd come to the revival. I didn't know what a revival was, but I imagined the girls from the lunch table sitting in the pews noticing I wasn't there.

I worried that I had disappointed these possible lunch-room...companions? Cohorts? Friends? Buddies? No! They were barely lunchroom contacts. I would never presume that we would ever be connected. I only hoped they wouldn't look at me suspiciously when I sat at their table. That was the best I hoped for.

I previewed the Monday morning scene in study hall. I imagined how they would look at me like I was a liar because I didn't go to their church Friday as I said I would. I played that scene over and over in my mind with many possible outcomes. None of these outcomes ever looked like forgiveness or acceptance.

When we pulled into our carport, I remembered that Dianne had said the revival would be going on until Sunday night. I guessed it would be OK for me to go. I really wasn't sure. But maybe I still had another opportunity to redeem myself from their speaking ill of me.

I asked Mama, "Can I go to a church meeting tonight? I heard about it at school." It was always a leap for me to hope for *anything*.

She looked at me puzzled. What a weird idea that I *wanted* to go somewhere without her, that I even *wanted* to go somewhere I wasn't required to go. It was unfamiliar to both of us.

"No, you can't go."

How could I face the girls the next day? "Please, I already told them I would go." Now Mama was even more puzzled. "Them?" I had a *them* in my life that wasn't connected with her?

But there was anxiousness in my voice, and she sensed a bargaining opportunity. "If I let you go, will you go to the grocery tomorrow to talk to them about that bad check they have? Tell them I'll pay them in a couple of weeks."

"Yes, Mama, I'll do it." *Please let me go.* My eye was on the prize: a table in the lunchroom where I would not feel rejected!

"You make sure you give them a good story about the check when you see them Monday."

"Yes, I will. Thank you Mama." I got back in the car, started the engine, and drove away. I was going to do something for me.

The church was a burnt orange brick building with the traditional steeple. I knew where it was because I passed it on the way to school. I drove into the parking lot filled with cars. It looked like all of the people were entering at a side entrance from where the steeple was. I walked in, trying to blend in with the crowd. I had walked directly into the back of the church.

There was Dianne sitting on the second-to-last pew. I slid in and sat next to her. She hugged me, "I'm glad you came." Thankfully, it was time for the service to start, so I didn't have to embarrass myself with social conversation.

At the close of the service, for reasons I could not understand, I began to tremble and then I began to cry. Dianne put her arm around me. It felt strange. I wasn't used to anyone showing me friendship.

When Dianne scooted out of the pew I followed her. I thought she was leaving the church or going to the restroom. I was not aware that we were still participating in the church service. Dianne went to the front, and I tagged along rehearsing my speech that I was going to give her when we got to the parking lot. The speech consisted of only five words, but it was important that I got it right. As we were getting in our cars to go home I would nonchalantly say, "See you at lunch tomorrow." I was now waiting for her to finish talking to the man at the front of the church.

That man turned out to be the visiting evangelist, and he turned and began talking to me. The first part of the conversation was confusing to me. He spoke church words I didn't understand. I honestly had no clue what he was talking about. I kept wondering why he was even talking to me. Out of politeness, I mumbled answers to his questions, but I really didn't understand him. I kept one eye on Dianne, so she wouldn't leave without me sealing the reason I had come.

Then another man. Fred Forrester, pastor of Northside Baptist Church, looked into my eyes with warm, loving, happy, fatherly eyes and said: "God loves you!" Instantly, I had a knowing that consumed me. At that very moment, my life changed forever! "God loves you!" It resounded in my ears; it pulsed through my whole body. All I could do was smile from ear to ear. I smiled with my whole heart. I didn't quite understand why, but I was bubbling happy. I was happy all over.

I forgot all about Dianne. The next thing I knew, I was introduced to the church. The pastor told them that I had gotten saved and joined the church, and I was going to be baptized. Well, I didn't realize I had joined the church. That wasn't my intention. I wasn't really sure what that meant. But, yeah, I guessed it would be OK. In the parking lot I didn't even think to give my speech to Dianne.

But what was I going to tell Mama? She was *not* going to like it that I had joined a church. I slowly drove up to the house. All the lights were off. Good! I went to our backyard and looked up in the sky. "God, You love me! You love me! I love You!" I stood there looking into the clear sky with the stars brightly glimmering. I felt at one with the heavens, overwhelmed with emotion and love for God. I didn't know what to do with all the happy, happy, happy emotions I felt. I started running around my house. After a couple of laps, I looked into the sky and said the same thing over and over again. "God, You love me! You love me! I love You!"

CHAPTER

SIX

THE NEXT DAY AT school I was greeted by "the gang." They all hugged me. "I heard what happened last night." "I heard you got saved last night." "Are you going to be coming to our church now?"

To say the least, I was dumbfounded. First, I didn't understand most of what they were saying about my salvation experience, and second, I was disoriented having people excited to see me and talk to me. But, I was smiling, not only with my lips but with my whole heart.

We lined up for lunch, and the chatter began. I was the center of it. I beamed at the cafeteria workers as they put food on my plate. I started crying because I was so ecstatically happy! Happy all over. When I got to the end of the line, the dreaded search for a table to sit at was over! I was part of a group now. They liked me. I knew it was because I went to church with them, but that was good enough for me!

They picked a table to sit at, and I kind of hesitated, just to make sure I had not misread their signals. Dianne looked up at me with those beautiful, big chocolate eyes and motioned for me to sit by her, "Over here." *Yes! Yes! I had lunch partners!* I experienced belonging in a light and happy way. That was contrasted to the heavy responsibility I felt belonging to the other world of Mama and me.

I was so out of character that day. I rambled on and interacted with my soon-to-become best friends. I found I could talk about God and how wonderful He was, and I didn't even have to search for the right words.

Of course, when the conversation shifted to anything else, I was at a complete loss. "Mrs. Brannon's English test was hard." "I made a B." I didn't have a clue how to be a part of that conversation. Although Mrs. Brannon was my favorite teacher and I thought she was very kind, I wouldn't dare risk making any sort of comment like that. I knew it would sound dumb coming from me! It didn't matter; I basked in all the wonderful new feelings I was experiencing.

I listened as the girls excitedly talked among themselves. I hoped they wouldn't direct any of that normal-world conversation to me. I didn't want to lose my lunch partners by them thinking I was a dud. *Lunch partner!* I didn't know it would feel this good. I looked around at many other conversational groups in the lunchroom. I thought, *If anyone looks at our table, I will look normal.* I knew my life wasn't normal, by a very, very long shot. But at least I could eat lunch in peace.

I loved having *friends*. It was great. There were about six girls who all hung out together at church, school, and out of school. I was part of the group. I remember getting that first phone call. It was Dianne. Her voice was dancing. "We're going to Frosty Inn to get a Coke. Can you come with us? We'll pick you up."

She was offering me the key to my prison. I wanted to reach out and grab it. No, I wanted to do more than that. I wanted to reach through the phone and hug her and hug her again, and thank her and thank her, and hug her once more and cry on her shoulder and never let her go! She had called and asked me a very simple question. She had no idea she was opening a whole new world to me.

"Yes, I would love to go!" I gave her directions to my house.

"I'll be there in thirty minutes."

Hmmm, thirty minutes. Mama was gone. Hopefully she would stay gone. What would I do if she showed up before Dianne got there?

Mama would not like it that someone from the church was taking my attention. She might throw a tantrum and say I couldn't go. But she didn't come home. My friends picked me up, and we laughed and talked and pulled into the parking lot like normal people. My heart was racing with happiness. I watched to see what the others ordered. June ordered a frosty mug of root beer. That sounded safe enough. Dreadfully self-conscious, I announced, "I'll have a medium frosty mug of root beer."

I couldn't wait to go to church again after that first Sunday night experience. The opportunity presented itself on the following Wednesday night.

I cried through the entire service. I loved the hymnbook. I loved the words in the hymnbook. I loved the music. I loved everything the kindhearted pastor said. I was still exuberantly happy!

When the service ended, I began to look around at all the things laid out in the back of the church. There were little folded papers that said "What We Believe." I picked up one of each of the papers on the table.

A lady walked up to me and called me by name. "Lana, let me give you one of these." She reached into a wooden rack on the wall. It had a handwritten sign over the top of it that said "Tract Rack." I wondered what that meant. She handed me one of the papers and said, "This is a story about someone who had an experience like you had at church Sunday night."

I took all my treasured papers home. I stayed up late that night reading and rereading. I liked the story of God's love on one of the tracts most. On the bottom of it was an address. It said, "For free tracts, write..." I mailed my request off the next day.

The following Sunday I was baptized in the church. Like the thief on the cross, my heart was open to God, and that one touch from Him transformed my life. My new friends gathered around me, as joyful as I was.

In about two weeks, I received a box full of tracts. They were printed on cheap off-white paper, and each tract was a story of how someone's life was totally changed by God's love.

Those simple stories took me into heaven. It was a world I'd never seen before. Life was terrible until God touched their lives. I learned about grace, love, forgiveness, salvation, and just how absolutely wonderful and perfect God is. I learned about how God loved me so much He gave His only Son, who died on the cross so all my sins could be forgiven.

At home I closed the door to my room and read the same box of tracts over and over. Mama opened the door and walked in my room. "Are you reading those papers *again*?" She was angry and resentful that I was totally absorbed in "those papers" and crying. "You need to clean up your room." There really wasn't anything to clean up. She was trying to draw me away from this new life I had found outside of her. I tried to explain it to her. She was totally uninterested. I knew she was drowning in her own addictions, and she feared my not being there for her.

She became increasingly irritated with my new friendships. "Why do you want to be with all those church people?" She saw them as a menace to our relationship, but I certainly didn't see it that way. God was in my life now, but the way I treated Mama did not change. I still took things back to the store for her. I still protected her when we were out. I still loved her more than any other person in the world.

I was drawn to the church library. I remember how I'd slipped into the library the first Sunday after the revival. Behind a desk was a friendly lady. I timidly walked around looking at the books. She recognized me from the Sunday before, when I had been introduced to the church. She stood up, hugged me, and welcomed me.

"Are you looking for something I can help you find?"

"I just want to learn about God."

She sweetly smiled at me. She took her soft little index finger and laid it on the spine of *The Robe*, a classic about the crucifixion of Christ.

"Is there a way I can take it home to read?" That was the first of many times Mrs. Richardson put her soft little finger on a book for me. At home I buried my head in it and slipped into a world I wanted to live in. At those times I was oblivious to the storms raging around me. I had lived alone in a desert with an unquenchable thirst. Now I kept drinking and drinking and drinking.

I joined the Sunday school class led by the pastor's wife, Mrs. Forrester. It turned out, she was the leader for the girls who were my friends. She was plump, wore glasses, and had salt-and-pepper hair. She loved to laugh.

Since I was at square one, I needed lots of tutoring. She lived in the parsonage next door to the church, and I found lots of excuses to call her. "Mrs. Forrester, can I come over and talk about last week's Sunday school lesson with you?"

"Yes, dear." I *loved* it that she called me "dear" in her motherly way. She hugged me with her plump arms when I got there and when I left. The feeling was something indescribable.

It was a happy, happy time.

Mama continued to want me by her side. To please her, I still stayed in the car outside bars for hours while she was inside drinking. Some of Mama's bar friends still came to the car to "check on me." I believe Mama was so consumed by her alcoholism and mental illness, she never even considered they might have other motives.

When the parade of faceless men came to the car now, I had a holy purpose and direction in my life. I had new power—strength from God and strength from having friends and strength from not being all alone. When I looked up at the faces outside the car window, I shook my head. When Frank unzipped his pants, God and I boldly said, "No, don't do that! Leave me alone! I'm reading my Bible." When I said that, they never stuck around.

My new life was a miracle.

CHAPTER
SEVEN

I WAS EAGER TO START college, but it was a foregone conclusion that I would not leave Mama. It was never even a consideration. Mama and I both had always laughingly said she would live with me even if I got married, so I had to go to a local college or not at all. Meanwhile, I had to earn the money to pay my tuition.

In the classified ads I read: "Secretary wanted for manager of new branch office in Baton Rouge. Experience preferred. Apply at Way and Brinks Refractories."

I drove to the office in Baton Rouge to apply. I had felt insecure and out of place for so much of my life that I should have been numb with fear, but I wasn't. I felt empowered by having God in my life. I spoke to Him all the time, telling Him everything. "Lord, if You want me to have this job," I prayed, "then I ask that You help me get it."

The interview room was filled with many other young women, and I was the last interview of the day. Mr. Way, the owner, and Mr. Talbot, the manager, interviewed me. Mr. Way said, "Everyone else who has applied has experience. Some of them have very good experience. Why do you think you can do this job with no experience?"

He didn't know my whole life had been on-the-job training for things I was totally inexperienced at doing. I had made bar drinks when I was nine, began driving when I was twelve, and covered up for Mama a hundred times. But of course I couldn't explain all of that to him, so I beamed with total self-confidence and said, "I know I can do it. I have no doubt. You'll not be sorry you hired me!"

After interviewing me for about twenty minutes, the two men stepped out of the room. When they walked back in, they looked at me and smiled. They looked at each other and smiled. Mr. Talbot said as he shook his head back and forth, "We are hiring you. It really is even a puzzle to us. You're the youngest one to apply. Out of the sixteen girls you're the only one with no experience. However, you have so much confidence, and you are such a delight to be around that the others don't even come close compared to you! Can you begin work Monday?"

I was so happy, all I could do was talk to God a mile a minute. *Thank You! Thank You! Thank You, Lord! That was not difficult at all with You by my side.*

In just a few short months, I had gone from being a stick-in-the-mud to being a leader in most everything I pursued. Even though inside, where no one else could see, I remained unstable and frightened in social interactions, on the outside, I looked poised and self-confident.

Within a year of joining Northside Baptist Church, I became president of the Young Women's Association. The YWA was the teen girl organization in the Baptist church. Our advisor, Mrs. Forrester, had connections with Louisiana College, the Baptist college about two hours north of us. She often said to me, "Lana, you would love attending LC. Please think about it."

She wouldn't understand that leaving Mama was not an option for me.

Dianne and I and most of our gang attended the YWA state retreat held at Tall Timbers in central Louisiana. By now Mama didn't say much about me flitting around to church functions. She reacted the way Mr. Talbot did when he gave me the job. She shook her head no but said, "Yes, you can go." It was a puzzle to her why I was so interested in "church stuff."

At the retreat I walked around in my own world with God, mesmerized by His presence. Marian McIntyre, the state YWA coordinator, asked to talk with me after one of the services. We talked for a long time on the cafeteria steps in the dark, except for a porch light.

I kept thinking, *Here I am, the former little dud conversing about God with the state coordinator.* It seemed like a miracle. She asked, "Are you going to college?" I explained to her my mother dilemma. She then asked a divinely inspired question that got my attention like nothing else would have: "Who is more important, God or your mother?"

It had never even entered my mind the possibility of being away from Mama again. Miriam continued, "If God wants you to go away to the Baptist college, He will take care of your mama."

The next morning we went to the big assembly room to conclude the retreat. The speaker's plane was delayed. Miriam looked out over the sea of girls crowded into the assembly hall and caught my eye. "Lana, would you come up front?" I was almost shaking as I walked to the stage. She had no idea how scary it was for me to be singled out, how much I wanted to blend into the wall whenever there was a crowd.

I stood beside her looking at all those people. *What am I doing? I don't belong here.* I heard her say, "While we're waiting for our speaker to arrive, I would like Lana to share her experience with God with all of you."

All fear dropped away. It was the one thing I could do. I could talk about Jesus all the time without ever feeling self-conscious or awkward. That morning I shared from my heart how good He is and how much He loves us. It was no effort to think of anything to say. It flowed easily.

The speaker finally arrived, gave her speech, and the retreat concluded. It had been fantastic! God's love was so profound, sometimes I felt I couldn't contain myself. As I left the assembly room, my friends rushed me to tell me how great I had done. Dianne was overjoyed. "That was wonderful," she said. "You didn't tell us you were going to be one of the speakers." Others said, "That was so good. How were you able to talk like that? I could never do that! You were so inspiring." All I knew was that God and I were a team, and the Holy Spirit strengthened me beyond my ability.

I began to make plans to go away to college. Mama would not hear of it. "No, you cannot go. I'll be so lonely."

"Mama, it will be OK. God will take care of you and me both."

She pouted, "You don't love me."

"Mama, I will only be two hours away. I can come home real often."

She cried, "You don't love me."

"Mama, you know I will always be just a phone call away." I hugged her and continued, "If I get a good education, I can get a good job to take care of us!"

"My little pumpkin, you are breaking my heart."

She was breaking my heart. Who did I love more? God or Mama?

"Mama, I have to go."

It took a few weeks of negotiating with Mama and praying for God to soften her heart. I applied for and was approved for a student loan.

Finally, I had one more day before I left. I dreaded telling her good-bye. I knew how hard it was going to be for her. *Oh, God, help me.* Then something unexpected happened.

We had a sickly dachshund named Sloopy that someone had given us. We had only had him about a year, but Mama had attached to him quickly. The day before I left, Sloopy died. Mama was so grief-stricken over the dog dying that she shifted her focus from me to the dog.

The night before I left, she slept with me. When my stepfather was working out of town, she often slept in my room. During the night I rolled over and must have tapped her with my foot. She sat straight up in bed and screamed, "Give me that knife. You're trying to kill me." She started throwing the covers off, looking for the knife.

The upset of the dog dying and her imagining that I had assaulted her took precedence in her mind over my abandoning her. As I pulled out of the driveway in my used Volkswagen, I waved and smiled to reassure her. I struggled to hold back the tears, and I know she did too. She stood in the doorway. "See you later, Pumpkin," she said.

Mama never said good-bye. That was too permanent. "No, don't say that!" she would tell me. "It sounds like you're going to die. Don't ever say good-bye! Say, 'See you later.'"

I watched her in my rearview mirror as I drove away. I watched her until I couldn't see her any longer with my eyes. I could see her in my heart, though. I never thought I would ever be the one to leave her. A few blocks from the house, I saw Northside Church, where my new journey had begun.

I pulled into the parking lot. I glimpsed at myself in the rearview mirror. I had long, straight brown hair. I still looked very plain. My eyes squinted when I smiled, which was most of the time now. Today, however, I was overcome with sadness as I imagined Mama at home crying and feeling abandoned. I burst out in tears! I don't know how long I sobbed on the steering wheel. "God, please take care of my mama! Please take care of my mama!"

Even though I cried, I did not mind leaving behind the daily trauma of her drinking, mental illness, and boyfriends. But because of my past, I was locked in an emotional prison I was yet to understand. No, I didn't leave Mama. She and all the pain that I had experienced were locked up deep inside of me.

CHAPTER

EIGHT

I HAD ONLY BEEN AWAY attending Louisiana College a few weeks when I received a surprising postcard. It was from my dad!

My dad. He never remarried, and I was his only child. I had only seen him briefly a few times after the divorce, but he wrote to me every few months. His return address was always different. Mama and I moved constantly, so it seemed normal to me that my dad also moved constantly.

I remember being so excited when he sent me a box of Russell Stover chocolate candy. He did that about four times. He would go in the candy shop and have them mail it to me. It connected me in some small way to this fantasy dad I had out there somewhere.

I didn't really understand when Mama talked about him. She told me, "He's paranoid schizophrenic. He hears voices. I don't know how he made it through WWII, and I certainly don't understand how he became a captain."

I found out from Aunt Daisy that my father had been a decorated war hero, having led troops at the Battle of Normandy on Omaha Beach. I listened intently as she talked about him. "He's very smart! He has a 162 IQ. Lana, the war really was hard on him. He doesn't say much about it."

Well, now I was going to find out for myself about my very own dad. I could hardly wait!

He was in a rooming house so rundown it must have been condemned. I carefully climbed the three flights of wobbly wooden stairs. My heart beat with anticipation at the thought of being with *my dad*. I knocked. No answer. I kept knocking. Finally, he fell against the door and opened it.

"Susan! Is that you? My very own daughter!"

Wow! I loved it that he called me by my real name, Susan. I loved the words "my very own" directed at me. My dad!

He had a receding hairline. I could see his blue, blue eyes, even through the extreme puffiness. He had high cheekbones and an olive complexion. I had never even dared to dream about a relationship with him. At his one statement, my heart fused with his. I was overjoyed at being with him.

I was so used to the bizarre that I didn't even flinch that he greeted me in only his boxer shorts. Also, he was drunk. I walked into a sparse room. There was a double bed and a few feet away a sink, a tiny icebox, and a counter with a hot plate on it. My learned behavior of rescuing shifted into high gear.

I fixed him scrambled eggs and ham. That was all there was in the icebox besides two six-packs of beer and a pound of butter. I made his bed and washed the few dishes.

I found out that when he traveled around, he carried a set of silverware, a small plate, bowl, can opener, and a frying pan. A typical transient, he bought his clothes at Goodwill. He wouldn't try them on. He guessed. So most of the time if the pants he bought were too small for him, he cut them at the waistline twice in front, twice in back. If he bought them too big, they were held up with numerous safety pins.

His shoes were stuffed with newspaper if they were too big or cut down the back at the heel if they were too small.

In his duffle bag, or "grip," as he called it, he generally had safety pins, canned Vienna sausage, rope to tie his pants up if need be, and his military records. Also included was religious literature, like a prayer book, paper hymnbook, and tracts he had picked up.

He often slept in the woods, in a park, or against the back of a building. He bathed in gas stations or park bathrooms. His mental illness, being shell-shocked in the army, and his alcoholism had all contributed to his transient lifestyle. Often he had money to get a room, but it was too scary for him to have to interact with people.

The room he was in provided the linens. He only had one sheet on the bed because he used the other for the window, even though it had a shade. I threw away the numerous empty beer cans, an empty wine bottle, his used bus ticket, candy wrappers, and one empty can of soup. He ate food directly from the can, so he probably had not warmed it.

I did not know before that day that he drank heavily. Actually, I knew nothing about him. But he was my dad! That was all I cared about. I had not the least bit of disappointment in him. I instinctively knew not to have expectations. If I had expectations, I would be hurt. It didn't matter, though, because I instantly loved him!

I went back to see him every day for three days. He was always drunk but nice to me. Each day I arrived, he greeted me the same way, "Susan, my very own daughter!" It warmed my heart to tears. Each day I cleaned his room and cooked for him. Together we made plans for me to come back the next day.

On the fourth day, I excitedly climbed the rickety stairs again. I didn't really care what condition I found him in or how the room looked. I wanted to be with him. That was all that mattered to me.

I knocked on the door. No answer. I kept knocking. An elderly, unshaven man came by and told me, "He moved out. Said he was catching a bus. Don't know where he went." More importantly, I didn't know where he went! I stood there motionless. This was the story of my life. There was no one I could depend on. He left me; I had been abandoned again. I had no idea if or when I would see him again.

I worked at the campus bookstore so I could pay my car note and other expenses. I was comfortable there. I loved handling books, even if they were mainly textbooks. I dated often. The main criterion I had in boyfriends was how much they loved God. I thought many of the preacher-wannabees I dated didn't seem to love God enough, though.

At Thanksgiving I called Mama and asked her, "Can I bring Stafford home for dinner? He's handsome. He's an administrator of two nursing homes that he is part owner of. He always wears a suit. He drives a Cadillac." I knew all this information would impress her. And it did!

She excitedly and laughingly said, "Bring your rich boyfriend home for Thanksgiving." I smiled to myself, *Yep. That is the way she would look at it.*

Stafford came from a stable home. His family was well respected in the Pineville community. I tried to prepare him to meet Mama. "Now, don't expect it to be a typical Thanksgiving."

Stafford parked his jade green Cadillac in front of our little gray brick house. By then, Mil had moved out and filed for a divorce, so it would be just the three of us. Mama came running out to greet us in her flamboyant, animated way.

"Pumpkin!" she exclaimed as she grabbed me and hugged me. She flirted with Stafford. "And you must be Staaafford!" She drawled out his name. I knew she meant nothing by it; she always talked to men in a flirtatious manner.

Mama rattled around in the kitchen and then came and set up our TV trays. No one was allowed to sit close to each other. She announced, "We are having baked duck and baked potatoes." Mama had always been very theatrical, and loved the shock effect. She watched for a response from Stafford.

She set a plate of duck in front of him. She put his baked potato on his TV tray. She walked around asking if he or I wanted salt or butter. Of course, each item had a date and time on it. She was the only one that could have control of these extra things.

Mama observed Stafford looking at his baked potato sitting on his tray. She said, "Wait, let me find a saucer. Hmmm, this will do. I can't find a saucer." She then shocked even me. She served Stafford his baked potato on a pot lid! Stafford had to choke back the laughter as we all bowed our heads and he gave thanks over our Thanksgiving meal.

I often wondered if Stafford told anyone about that unusual day.

One day Mama showed up at the college with her new boyfriend, Leslie, who was twenty years younger than she. They were intoxicated. I led them away from the dorm to a restaurant where no one knew me. While Leslie flirted with me, Mama plotted the con she was about to spring.

"Pumpkin, my car is not running. That's why I had to ride with Leslie to come see you. Let me borrow your car for a few days. When mine is fixed I'll bring it back." I wasn't sure if any of that was true. However, when Mama wanted something from me, I always gave in to her whims and wishes. That's how it had always been. As she drove my car away, I should have known I'd never see it again.

Mama called me a couple weeks later. "Pumpkin, I had a wreck. LeRoy and I were at that bar, Teenie's. We left about midnight. I hit the bridge and totaled out your car."

"Mama, were you hurt?"

"No, but I was forty miles from home. I left your car on the side of the road and called a cab. I left LeRoy's sorry self there too. I didn't have any money to give the cab driver. It was about two o'clock in the morning when we got close to the house."

I could already guess what was coming. We had been through so much together, I knew her inside and out. "I had the cab driver pull in a driveway about two blocks from the house. I told him I would go in and get the money. I went through the backyard of several houses to get home." She laughed with great satisfaction at having been smart enough to pull a fast one on the cab driver. "I guess he's still waiting for his money, and I guess your car is still sitting on the side of the road! It happened last week. I'm surprised no one has called you about it."

I never got angry with her about my car or the cab driver. This was all I had ever known.

I prayed for Mama unceasingly, "Lord, save her! Free her from alcoholism. Protect her." I realistically could not see Mama changing. When I prayed for her, I imagined her having a deathbed experience, like the thief on the cross. With her dying breath she would turn her life over to God. This was the best I could hope for!

The next time I went home to see Mama, she was living in Madisonville, Louisiana. Her new boyfriend, Ralph, bought her a bar and café and put it in her name. I stayed at Ralph's while I was visiting her. Leslie, her younger boyfriend, was living there, too. Mama told Ralph that Leslie needed to rent a room for a short while. That crazy arrangement with two boyfriends under one roof lasted a year.

CHAPTER
NINE

I HAD LIVED IN THE midst of insanity for seventeen years with no resources. Now I spent my free time involved in church or frequenting the Bible, Book and Record Store. I soaked in every sermon, every book, and every conversation, anything that would teach me another way of life.

The owner was Mrs. Davis. She was thin, tall, and wore her dark hair twisted up in a bun. She wore narrow, dark-rimmed glasses. My requests were pretty much the same when I went into the bookstore: "Can you recommend a record for me to buy?" "Can you recommend a book to teach me a closer walk with God?"

I bought about twenty-five books from her my first year in college. One of my favorite authors was Andrew Murray. He and authors similar to him challenged me to have a heart-to-heart relationship with Jesus.

My dorm roommate, Pam, was used to me disappearing in the evening. "I'm going up to the vacant room on the third floor to listen to my gospel records." I loaded up my cheap little record player, my records, Bible, and books and went to my quiet place. I liked being alone. I cried and hung on to every word of the music. I got lost in adoration for the One who had completely transformed my life. I could not get enough of the presence of God.

One day while I was browsing in the bookstore, Mr. Davis, who owned a wholesale company, Gospel Book and Music Distributors, asked, "Lana, would you come and work for me?" He took me by surprise. All of the many books and records about God she distributed had become a major part of my life. It was like being asked to live in Disneyland. I didn't even have to know what the job was. "Yes!" I exclaimed.

I worked off and on for Mr. Davis for three wonderful years.

Sometimes I worked one and two jobs while going to college. Sometimes I stayed out of college simply to work.

I took a leave from college and moved to Lafayette, Louisiana. There I worked for a federally funded community poverty program doing social work. My work partner, Allison, and I went to the homes of lower-income people. We gave them information to help them network with programs that could help them.

I loved working with those who needed my help. One rainy day, Allison and I knocked on a client's door.

Mrs. Richard came to the door wearing a shapeless brown dress. She had a shy look about her, but she invited us into a tiny, dismal living room. I noticed two coffee cans in the middle of the room, set up to catch rainwater. I began, "Mrs. Richard, we would like to share with you the various programs that are available to you in our community. If you would allow us, we will fill out a brief questionnaire. We then can see which programs you qualify for so we can get you some assistance."

"Y'all come on in the kitchen and we can sit at the table and talk."

We walked from the living room through the one bedroom to the kitchen. All together, there were only three rooms and a bath.

I nodded to Allison to ask the questions while I discreetly looked around. I felt so sad for this lady that I had to hold back tears. They were like a dam ready to burst. I wanted to help her. No, I needed to help her. When I saw a need, I felt responsible to help fix it.

I asked, "How many live here?"

Mrs. Richard explained, "Me and my three little children. Me and Josie sleep in the bed, and Elsa and Mattie sleep on the couch, each on one end." She pointed to a broken-down, under-stuffed couch.

I didn't say anything to Allison, but after work I went to Home Furniture. I told Andy, the salesman, "I need to buy a couch for a poor family. Two children will be sleeping on it." I'd seen a sign in the window: Zero Interest for Six Months. That meant that I could pay it out in six months.

He suggested, "Here's a nice sleeper sofa."

"No, the living room's not big enough to open it up." Andy showed me a sturdy brown-and-tan tweed couch. "I will take this one."

I went to the Christian bookstore and bought a little wooden plaque with roses painted on it. It said, "God loves you." It only cost three dollars, but that was all I could afford.

I went back to Mrs. Richard's house. "I'm sorry to bother you again, but we bought you a new couch that will be delivered tomorrow."

She grabbed me and hugged me, "Oh, how wonderful! Thank you so much!" I handed her the plaque. "Will it be OK if I say a little prayer with you?"

She pulled me into her house. "Yes, yes, that would be nice. Oh, look how pretty this picture is! You know, I love roses! I'll hang it right by my new couch!"

And so I prayed with her, "Lord, I ask for You to be with Mrs. Richard and her children. I ask that as they sit on and lie on their new couch they will be reminded how much You love them. I ask that they will wake up each morning feeling a little more secure in Your care for them. Amen."

I didn't want to tell Mrs. Richard that I had bought the couch. I think she assumed the agency did that for her.

My experience with Mrs. Richard was not unusual. When I went into the homes of the people in my territory and saw the deplorable conditions some of them lived in, my heart and mind immediately wanted to make a difference in their lives. I loved helping people, and I desperately wanted to rescue them as I had rescued Mama a thousand times.

I visited Andy at Home Furniture many more times to purchase a sofa or bed for one of our clients. I am not sure how I could afford all that I was doing. However, my only expense was upkeep on a broken-down car and rent on a meager apartment.

Mama's life was still chaotic. She got married one more time. That didn't work out. She had a violent fight with another boyfriend, who cut her up with a razor blade. I went running home each time. I knew it was my job to protect her, so I made her an offer. "Mama, if I try to support you, will you quit having boyfriends?"

I think she was relieved not to have to depend on men for financial support, but she never told me that. We just eased into our new arrangement. Besides paying her bills, I gave her a gas credit card.

After about three months of paying an extremely high credit card debt for Mama, I passively asked, "Mama, our Amoco gas bill shows charges everyday. Do you think that's correct?"

She unashamedly said, "Oh, I just go to different stations that I know and ask them for cash. They write it on the charge ticket as gas." That was it. No apology. No concern for me. That was our normal, matter-of-fact relationship. We were both used to it.

By then I was twenty-four. Our relationship was so entangled that if she fell in a ditch I still dropped everything and ran to her side to help her out. I had spent so much time in her daily trauma that my college studies took second place. Actually, all my needs took second place to doing whatever was needed for Mama.

As I explained earlier, I dropped out of school regularly to work. When I was ready to go back to school, I moved to another area and resumed my studies at a different university. I was used to moving around constantly. I also was very uncomfortable with relationships. It was easier for me to move away then to experience the trauma of trying to fit in.

One weekend after I had started yet another college, I went home to visit Mama. We went to the Sunflower grocery store. "I'm going to the liquor section," she told me. I knew not to bother her. I figured she would spend fifteen to twenty minutes there examining the seal on the bottle cap. It had to be perfect or she would fear it had been tampered with.

That day it seemed like she spent an unusually long time buying her Scotch. She was by that time drinking a fifth and a half a day. I often wondered how she could even physically consume that much. She never had been a binge drinker.

Finally, I saw her move her basket to the checkout line. I went over to the liquor department to see how much her bottle of Cutty Sark was, since I was paying most of the bills. The price tag said $15.63. She was buying it by the half-gallon now.

I caught up with her at the register. The half-gallon she purchased had a price label on it for $11.21. She had changed the price sticker! Fear gripped me. I imagined the police coming and arresting her. What would she do if she were locked up? Of course, I never said anything to her. I never did.

Driving back to college, a feeling of panic came over me. I realized this was an ongoing behavior and that she had a good possibility of being discovered. I was the little girl God had given her to protect her, but I had lost control. I couldn't protect her from this flagrant violation!

That night I had a psychology class. Sitting in the back of class, I began to cry while my teacher lectured. I cried quietly through the whole class, trying to be unnoticed. I left the class, still in a panic mode. I didn't know what to do. I thought I was cracking up. I had no one to call because I still hadn't let anybody into Mama's and my world.

I had never spoken to my psych professor, but in desperation I hunted in the phonebook for his name and called him. I blurted out, "My mom's an alcoholic. I have been trying to take care of her financially, and now something has happened. I think she may go to jail. I don't know what to do!"

That was the bottom line. I didn't know what to do! I had always had some reasoning skills to protect and shelter her.

He kindly said, "Let's meet for coffee tomorrow." That gesture by this caring professor was the beginning of the end of the life I had always known. He connected me with Jean, an outpatient alcoholism counselor. I made weekly appointments to see her for about three months.

Jean spoke directly to my situation. It was the first time I had heard anyone talk about alcoholism. She was the first person, the first resource, I had ever had to deal with Mama's alcoholism.

All of my problem-solving skills had been instinctive. My reason for existing was to tend to Mama. This was what had helped me survive.

Jean gently told me, "You bail her out of jail for a DWI. You're attentive to her every want and need. Lana, you're enabling your mother to drink. You have good intentions, but you're helping to trap her in a vicious circle of relief and defeat."

She asked me a question I had never considered: "What consequences does she have for recklessly drinking?"

I felt embarrassed and sheepish. "I don't know."

I was Mama's caretaker. I thought I did a good job at it. How could it be that I was part of the problem?

Talking to Jean made me understand the reality I lived in with my mama was distorted and twisted. Because of all my past fears of abandonment, I had a high tolerance for her inappropriate behavior. I had never even considered that our lives could change.

Jean counseled, "Let your mama take responsibility for her actions. Break the cycle." Her advice was drastic. How could I possibly limit Mama in any way?

As I began to process this new information, I read all the books Jean recommended to me. I came to understand that Mama had an obsessive-compulsive mental illness. Jean said, "Your mama probably has so much anxiety from her illness that she self-medicates herself with alcohol. The untreated mental illness led to her alcoholism, which is her coping mechanism."

Jean advised, "Lana, quit acting like a one-person rescue squad! Let her take some responsibility for her behavior. Begin by taking the credit card away from her."

I felt definitely that this was what God was leading me to do, but it took almost two more years before I was able to make that big leap. I rehearsed my plan, and then God and I went home and talked to her about it. "Mama, I just cannot afford any longer to pay our bills. I need to take the gas credit card back. I will buy you a trailer. I will pay the rent to park it, and I will pay the utilities. I will give you an allowance for the rest." I was gentle but firm. Mama didn't say anything. She knew it was a foregone conclusion.

We generally didn't talk about real-life situations anyway, so it wasn't out of the ordinary that we didn't discuss this new arrangement. I thought she probably felt the way I did. If we talked about real life and drew attention to our daily drama, neither one of us would be able to cope with it. We both lived in the reality of our own insanity. Mama's life didn't look like that of "normal" people I knew, and my limitless caretaking of her didn't look like that of "normal" people I knew, either!

Meanwhile, in the Bible I read that God did unusual and extraordinary miracles through Paul. Handkerchiefs that Paul prayed over were sent to sick people, and they were healed and made whole. I didn't know anyone who had tried this, but the minister I was dating, a nice guy named Howard, was familiar with the practice.

I bought Mama a flowered mother-looking handkerchief.

Howard and I traveled to the Teaching Center in Lafayette and got two other ministers there to pray over the handkerchief with us. As the four of us prayed for my mother's salvation and freedom from alcohol, I knew that I knew there was something different about this time of prayer.

A few days later, I went to her new trailer and gave it to her. "Mama, we held this handkerchief in our hands and prayed for you. It's kind of like the prayers are with you now. It's not magic. It's to remind you that we are praying for you and that God is with you and He loves you." I handed her the handkerchief.

She held it to her chest as if it were a lifeline. "I'm going to put it in my pillowcase. I'll sleep on it every night."

I bubbled over when I told people, "This is it. My mom's going to be free of alcohol. I just *know* it." Nothing could deter me. God had dropped a gift of faith in my heart concerning the prayers over this little handkerchief. A couple weeks later, I took the credit card away.

Next, Mama said she needed to go to the hospital for her nerves. Mama took her handkerchief to the hospital with her, and she sneaked her padlocked tackle box of Scotch into the hospital. This was her security until they could give her anti-depressants and anti-anxiety medication. When they gave her pills, she always asked for the maximum, and then she stockpiled them. She drank her Scotch the whole time she was there. When she figured she had enough pills, she would try to taper off the drinking at her own rate while she was in the hospital. She could not risk going into withdrawal. Of course, she never divulged to the medical staff that she was an alcoholic. I don't believe she even admitted that to herself!

One morning, the entire hospital wing was in an uproar. Mama had lost her handkerchief! It had become her lifeline, her point of contact. She kept it in her pillowcase. I believe this had become her private meeting place between God and her. She was like a drowning person, lost in a sea of bizarre confusion, hopelessness, and anxiety, spiraling downward in the vortex of life. Her only anchor was gone.

"When they changed my bed, the housekeeper took my handkerchief in my pillowcase." She solicited all the help she could get from nurses, aides, anyone that was in earshot. "Go down to the laundry and find my handkerchief." She was not mean about it, just determined.

They found it!

Mama got out of the hospital with meds for anxiety. We never used the words *sober* or *alcohol*, but I know she put her head on her pillow that contained her handkerchief and prayed for God to help her stay sober.

Within a few days she began to drink again. It lasted two days. She went back in the hospital with her handkerchief. When she came out, she never drank again!

Chapter

TEN

WHAT IF I HAD *my own bookstore? What would it look like?* I thought about it, dreamt about it, prayed about it. That was all it was, though, a thought, a dream, and the prayer of a young woman who had attended four universities, held eleven jobs, moved twelve times, and had had twenty-one boyfriends.

I had observed Mr. and Mrs. Davis in their businesses, wholesale and retail. I was a bookkeeper, packer, shipper, and did just about anything else they needed.

Then one day while I was browsing through the books at a Christian bookstore, something I can't explain welled up inside me. I was ready to have my own store. As soon as I got home, I grabbed a pencil and a brown paper bag. There, sitting at a small wooden table with my feet propped on the other chair, I began to plan. Overflowing with hope and enthusiasm, I wrote out budgets for all I would need to open a store of my own.

I could clearly see the store that I was certain God had destined for me. I could see people from all over the community coming in for help and for resources. I could see myself able to put just the right thing in their hands. The more I planned, the more settled I became in my heart.

All my effort was focused now. But I wasn't in a hurry. I wasn't even sure where it would be or when it would be, but I knew it would be soon. I tweaked the numbers regularly, reassessed them, and made adjustments to my plans. In other towns I visited other bookstores to see what I liked or didn't like.

My list of expenses included rent, utilities, supplies, and equipment, and then the big one—inventory. In my head I saw a shelf of Bibles, six racks of books, gospel music, greeting cards, and gifts. I saw inexpensive, small items that had inspirational sayings on them. Maybe I could give them away to anyone who needed an encouraging word. I didn't know how I could get the money to do all this, but I was 100 percent sure that the team of God and I could make it work.

Daily He and I spoke in conversational prayer. He was my Best Friend. My life revolved around Him. I didn't want to leave His side. When I did take the wrong path and separated myself from Him, I cried out, "I want You. I'm sorry." My life's passion was to be close to God.

Brother Sidney Fontenot and his wife, Delores, pastored Faith Temple in Sulphur, Louisiana, about seventy-five miles west of Lafayette. I had become close to them. I had spoken in their church and stayed in their home many times. Because I had no roots and didn't care where I lived, I made a decision: I would move to Sulphur, and that's where I would have my bookstore.

There were plenty of places to sit in church, so when a young man introduced himself as Michael and asked in a soft-spoken voice, "Can I sit with you?" it was apparent he wanted to get to know me. He was 6'3" and weighed 210 pounds. He had dark hair and wore old-fashioned, small, black-rimmed glasses with thick lenses.

I was already dating two guys and really wasn't interested in seeing anyone else, but I moved over and said, "Sure."

After church, Michael politely asked, "Would you like to go out sometime?" I wasn't good at saying no and I hated to hurt anyone's feelings. He didn't seem to be my type, but I said, "Yes, that would be great."

"Can I pick you up for church tonight?"

Well, that was fast. I stared at him wondering why he didn't get more stylish glasses, or at least something that matched his stature. They were way too small for his face.

Michael began picking me up for church regularly. I learned that he attended Bible school and hoped one day to go into the ministry. His relationship with God was his number one passion. That instantly attracted me to him.

Mike was always neat and clean but unmatched and wrinkled. His favorite thing to wear for almost a year of our dating was a wrinkled orange knit shirt with a wrinkled brown knit print pair of pants. He had a small wardrobe of three outfits. He didn't think he needed any more clothes. When his three outfits got dirty, he washed them at the Laundromat and shoved them into his laundry bag with his other laundry necessities. He seemed to be a typical bachelor to me.

Meanwhile, my plan to open the Christian bookstore met with a huge barrier. There was a store already in Sulphur. The Good News Bookstore owned by Mr. Guillory was a combination of Christian books, secular books, used books, coins, and drugstore items. As badly as I wanted to open a store, it was not even a slight option for me to compete with Mr. Guillory.

Instead of opening my own store, I went to work at the Christian Book Center in Lake Charles. One of the people that came into the store regularly was Judy Elaine. She often bought tracts to give away. I shared with her my plans to open my own Christian bookstore. She said, "I've always wanted to open a bookstore, too. Let's do it together."

I had only been dating Michael about six months when he asked the one question I was not ready for. "Will you marry me?"

"I can't." I explained to him that I had a single destiny at this time, and it was a bookstore.

But we continued to date, and he continued to ask me to marry him. We had lots of fun together talking about spiritual things. We really didn't talk about anything else. We were both single-minded in our pursuit of God.

Then something I call a God-incidence happened. We were visiting after church with Mike's cousin, Clara, when she said, "I'm quitting my job as the manager of the Good News Bookstore in Sulphur."

I exclaimed, "Clara, I am going to apply for your job as manager!"

I went to see Mr. Guillory. "I want to apply to be your manager." Before he could even respond, I blurted out, "Would you be interested in selling your store?"

He was as startled as I was. "Yes, I sure am!"

God's destiny in me bubbled over. I was ready.

I told Judy Elaine of my plan. She was persistent that she also wanted to open a store, so we agreed to go into business together. She would continue working at her job in visual merchandising, and I would manage and operate the store.

The Son Shine Shop opened when I was twenty-eight years old.

The first exciting day of business, Bitsy, a long-time, prominent resident in the community, came in to welcome me. She had that sweet, motherly look big time! I felt overjoyed. All was going well, and then she asked two innocent questions: "Where are you from? Who is your family?"

I had often encountered this intrusion into something I did not want to talk about. On the outside I smiled sweetly and said that all of my mom's family was from Hammond, then I quickly diverted the conversation to something else. But on the inside I was still that little girl hovering in the corner of life. *Don't anyone notice me.*

When Bitsy asked me those questions, I emotionally threw on the brakes and became guarded.

On the outside there was no change. I kept smiling, but inside I pulled into what I thought was my true self. I went back into my lost world. *I don't fit, I don't belong,* I reminded myself. The rest of the day, a black cloud hung over me. Who did I think I was trying to integrate into society? I thought I would be safe in this God-and-me business world. But then sweet, innocent Bitsy came and wanted to know more of my life. I was totally inept at sharing that part with anyone.

That first night the new store was open I cried in my pillow. "God, help me. Help me to do Your will. You have given me the passion, enthusiasm, and knowledge to do this. I know I deserve nothing and I am nothing. For Your honor and glory alone, help me to block out who I am." It would be many years before my wrong thinking came to light.

But, joy comes in the morning, and I woke up the next morning with passion, enthusiasm, and knowledge burning in me once again. I was invigorated just thinking about the multitude of people that would have a personal encounter with God because of our Bibles, books, music—everything.

I loved the store! The business! Being an entrepreneur! I whizzed through the business end of the store, buying, selling, planning, taking risks. I was a natural at it. It was a hand-in-glove fit for me. I loved God! I loved resources! I wanted to help people find God like I had.

We bought cases of books by Andrew Murray to give away. I loved putting just the right thing in people's hands. I was just as happy whether they paid for it or if I gave it to them.

I remember Jim, one who, like many others, came in the bookstore discouraged. "Miss Lana, I feel like I am letting God down. I don't feel close to Him." I gave him *Abide in Christ* by Andrew Murray.

He came back in the store three weeks later to tell me his story. "I reluctantly began reading the book you gave me. I never heard anything like that. Even though I've been in church most of my life, I see now I never really had my own experience with God. I knew about Him, but I didn't know Him personally for myself."

Jim reached across the counter and took my hand and shook it. "Thank you for being there when I needed you!"

Today I still meet people who tell me how much *The Son Shine Shop* changed their lives. "You know the books you gave me caused me to hunger for a deeper relationship with God." "*Abide in Christ* changed my life." "I didn't know He really loved me!" I still hear those stories. I know they are true!

We were the one-stop shop for spiritual resources in Sulphur. I didn't have to think about the lost little girl inside of me. I was in my element!

Mama did not gracefully recover from her alcoholism. For years she had self-medicated her phobias with the huge amount of alcohol she consumed daily. She was drinking one and a half fifths of liquor a day by the time she quit. Alcohol had been her coping mechanism for all her adult life.

Then her lifetime pattern of getting through the present moment by using alcohol was eliminated. I could see her mounting anxiety, and I was almost as anxious as she was. We both fumbled around to calm her panic attacks as she tried to adjust to anti-anxiety medication. "Lord, please help her. Please help her. Please help me to help her!"

I visited her often during this adjustment period to reassure her and check on her. She was so unhappy and mixed up. I asked, "Mama, are you satisfied with the medications you are taking?"

Her nerves were stretched, and she snapped at me, "Pumpkin, can't you see? I'm trying real hard for this to work!" She was anxious, irritable, and fearful.

Her ritualistic routines that comforted her in the past were disrupted as well. `I watched her nervously at the sink washing and washing ice to fix her beverage of the day. She changed her patterns as fast as she decided on them.

"I thought I could drink 7-Up, but then I changed to fruit punch. Now I think I like orange juice best. I have been drinking tea some, too." She kept rambling almost incoherently about the many drinks she had tried to settle on.

"Pumpkin, what do you think I should drink?"

She bought six-packs of juice, drank one, then changed to something else the next day. When I visited her, she gave me boxes of abandoned drinks to take home.

I was terrified that one day I would come into her home and smell the alcohol again, so it was always a huge relief when I found her still experimenting with her other beverages. A huge financial burden had been lifted as well.

However, the reasons she had been drinking were not resolved. Her mental illness didn't stop when she stopped drinking. It erupted worse than ever. She had a fanatical obsession with trying to find a replacement for her past rituals.

Her handkerchief continued to be her lifeline. Whenever I was with her, I held it and prayed for her salvation and peace. "Pumpkin, I keep it in my pillow case at all times." If Mama had voiced what I knew she was feeling, she would have said, "I'm terrified!" But we had never talked, ever, about our feelings.

After three months of sobriety, she began to have hallucinations. I called her doctor and told him, "I'm afraid my mother is losing her mind. I'm scared. I don't know what to do! Is it the medication?"

He tried to calm me down, reassuring, "She's going through alcohol withdrawal. I don't know if you're aware of how serious your mother's mental and physical illness is. Without medication, she literally cannot deal with the fears she's experiencing. This is a brain disorder. She cannot help herself."

Finally, Mama found an odd sort of help, a new ritualistic behavior. I could remember Mama regularly at a sink running water to rinse her ice for a drink and fussing over her bottle of Scotch. She now took her tiny new medication pills and somehow quartered them. So, instead of taking medications three times a day, she could take them twelve times a day, one-fourth of a pill at a time! She maintained her same rituals at the sink but substituted the elements.

I could see her alcohol-induced fog begin lifting slowly.

Dad was in town, coming and going in my life. I loved every minute I was with him. I missed not growing up with him. I found out he had stayed in touch with Mama through the years, mainly to harass her about me living in bars.

He frequently heard voices that haunted him, and he believed the world was against him. The sad part for me was that often the voices he heard told him I wanted to hurt him.

But there were times when he didn't lose touch with reality. I cherished the moments we could just be dad and daughter.

He drove up to the bookstore and surprised me. Since I was used to his bizarre comments, I wondered what he would say as I showed him around. He looked at everything in the store with a proud expression. "Susan, look what you have done. President Carter will be coming to visit you. He wants to see what you are doing here. He will probably give you a citation of recognition for the great work you are doing!"

I feared responding the wrong way. I might set him off. So I pretty much just ignored the strange comments he made.

While Dad looked around the shop, the phone rang. He hated that. His paranoia caused delusions of persecution. He growled, "Don't tell them I'm here." I answered the phone, "The Son Shine Shop. Jesus loves you."

The voice on the other end was panicky. "Yes, I was just in your store. I'm next door using the phone. I was scared of that man in your shop. He kept looking at me strangely. I'm calling to see if you're all right and if you want me to call the police."

"Thank you so much for calling. Everything's OK." I did not want to embarrass her by telling her the strange man was my dad.

Sometimes the peculiar things he did as a result of his mental condition made me laugh. I loved him and adored him and only laughed to myself in an endearing way. He was my dad. He had a 162 IQ. He was a highly decorated captain in WWII. I was proud of him.

Dad had a great sense of humor. One day I asked, "How are you doing?" He responded, "Not so good, since the accident. Someone offered to buy me a drink, and I accidentally didn't hear him!"

He was always chasing down his VA check. He moved so much, it couldn't keep up with him. Of course, in his thinking, the head of the CIA stole it, or the postal clerk, or the bank, or me, or Mama.

When he was in town, I picked him up and took him to the grocery store or the post office or wherever he needed to go. We were on Main Street, right by my bookstore, and out of the clear blue he rolled down his window and began to yell, "Help me, help me, help me. She won't let me out. Somebody help me. Please help me." I sped up and took him home before he jumped out of the car.

Being with him was like flipping channels on a TV. I had no idea when the channel would be changed and what I would be watching next.

Once when we were in the grocery store, I went down a different aisle than he did. Then I couldn't find him. I went up and down the aisles looking for him, wondering where he could be, wondering how I had missed him. Then I thought, *Maybe he's waiting for me outside in the front.* I looked outside, and there he was at the other end of the parking lot on the phone.

I raced over to him and asked, "Dad. What are you doing?"

"I'm calling a cab." He was determined to get to the bus station and go to California. He did things like this numerous times. The voices told him of some farfetched threatening development, and he would flee. The first few times this happened, I didn't know what to do or what to think. I had no security that I would ever see him again. Eventually, I shifted gears and understood that this was normal for my dad.

Normal for Dad would be weird if other people did it. More than once, while taking him places, he angrily turned around in his seat and questioned, "Susan, who are you hiding on the floorboard in the back?" If he thought I had said something threatening to him, he hauled off and backhanded me while I was driving.

But what hurt me most was that neither one of my parents trusted me. Even though I knew it was due to their illnesses, it still hurt. I was the only one they could depend on, but yet they feared me. I jumped through hoops so my parents could feel secure in my love for them, but I don't know how much they were ever able to grasp.

There was only one thing I could do. I tucked the sadness away and prayed, *Lord, please protect them. Give me wisdom day by day to deal with them.*

I could not have loved them any more if they had been perfect parents. I would do anything I was capable of for them. My personal pain or wants and desires were never an issue when it came to sacrificing for Mama and Dad.

But there was to come a time when God would no longer let me bury my hurt. He would no longer allow me to hide from all the pain that simmered below the surface.

CHAPTER
ELEVEN

W
HEN MY FRIEND, BETH, breezed into the bookstore that morning, I couldn't have guessed the major turn my life was about to take. "Lana, I really want you to come to my house for an organizational meeting for the Sulphur Women's Aglow Fellowship."

Oh no! I had no idea what she was talking about, and it sounded way too social for me. But since I didn't know how to say no politely, I agreed. "Yes, I guess I can come," I responded.

Walking into Beth's beautiful two-story contemporary home, I instantly felt out of place. Attractive and sophisticated-looking ladies seemed to fill her living room. There I was, plain, gawky, and homely. I sat down, but I did not belong.

Beth introduced a woman named Judy Robinson, who explained that Women's Aglow was a national organization of Christian women who met monthly to invite other women to hear the good news of Jesus. Aglow was open to all denominations and to women who had no church at all. It was growing in numbers rapidly across the country.

Judy wanted to start a chapter in Sulphur. She explained the dynamics. "Women's Aglow will meet once a month. We'll have a guest speaker who will share her experience about Jesus or speak on a spiritual subject. You have been invited here so we can select hostesses, chairmen, and two more officers."

After a time of prayer, she handed out pieces of paper and asked us to write down in what capacity we felt God wanted us to serve.

Judy had perfect blonde hair. She was stunningly beautiful and seemed totally together, a gifted leader with a winsome personality. My palms perspired and my stomach knotted. *I do not fit in with this group of women at all. I am a perfect dud compared to them!*

Judy kept talking. "There'll be lots of opportunity for bonding among ourselves and the women attending our meetings." That was the last thing I wanted. Relationships were not opportunities. They were weighty responsibilities. I wrote a few words on the paper: "I can help clean up."

Judy dismissed the meeting. "We will be in prayer concerning where God wants each one to fit into the group." I felt relieved to get out of there, to get back to my bookstore and to my safe boyfriend, Michael.

That afternoon, Judy called me. "After much prayer, we feel like God has selected you to be one of the officers on our board." I had no idea how to respond. *She would expect me to be excited, I guess.*

But I didn't know how to feel excited. When people are opening their gifts at Christmas and they get something really cool and say, "Oh, wow! Thanks! This is so awesome!"—I could never act like that. I was impaired emotionally. That was the leg that had been chewed off. Although people often commented on me smiling all the time, deep down I was completely solemn and fearful. The smile they saw was my genuine, overflowing love for God because I lived in a world with Him. But I did not live easily in a world of people.

I responded to Judy in my usual, flat way. "OK." That was all I could think to say. It seemed rude when she was so gracious, but that was the best I could do. I know I made her feel awkward, but she said, "Why don't you pray about it and get back with me."

God, You know I feel like I don't belong or fit with those ladies. But is this something You want me to do? I can't figure this out on my own. Help me. I began to feel in my heart that God wanted me to be a part of this Women's Aglow chapter. I called Judy back and nervously told her, "Yes, I will." That was it; I didn't know what else to say. I felt like the response needed more than that, but I was clueless.

The following week I joined Judy and three other women, Beth, Christine, and Kay, for our first board meeting. They all seemed gentle and kind and competent—and ritzy and sophisticated. I hardly opened my mouth. All I could do was pull myself in with God.

They actively talked about themselves and the upcoming meeting we were planning. I observed and listened, motionless, as if watching a play on a stage. I cautiously entered in only when spoken to. While smiling at them, I stayed in an intense inner conversation with God. *Why am I here, God? You know I'd do anything for You. You know I love You, but I don't belong.*

I spoke only when I felt God gave me something to say. As I sat there, I sensed God wanted me to speak up concerning our first speaker. We had several names we were discussing but couldn't settle on just the right one. But before I could say anything, I had to rehearse it a couple of times before speaking up. In a stiff voice I said, "I don't know Jeanne Woody, but after everything that you've said, I feel like she is the one we should ask."

Judy and the rest of the board chimed in, "Yes, you're right. OK, let's call Jeanne."

The board had wonderful prayer times each day for a full week before our monthly meeting. I did well with that. The part that I could not get used to was the socializing. We took our speaker out the night before our meeting to a fancy restaurant and invited our chairman and hostesses to join.

The first time was like the second time and like the third time and on and on. Just like it had been in high school and college, if we talked about God, I could flow in the conversation easily. But as soon as someone talked about shopping or her family, I felt this familiar, stabbing pain of hurt in my chest. I dug my heels in, in a self-imposed rejection. *I don't belong; I don't fit.*

Although my life was absolutely committed to God, I had trapped myself in destructive, negative talk. I wanted to serve Him more than anything, but I was still locked in an emotional prison: a little barroom girl who did not belong with "normal" people. Nine more years would go by before I could be free.

Meanwhile, Women's Aglow had much to teach me.

The phone was ringing. I fumbled around to answer it. The digital clock said 2:15 a.m. "This is the San Francisco Police Department. I am calling for Susan."

At first, all I could think was, *Oh, no! Dad?* I responded to the officer, "This is Susan."

"We have your father here at the police station. One of the police officers was patrolling in the Golden Gate Park, and he found your dad sleeping in the park. It's forty-three degrees here. He's only wearing a T-shirt. We were initially arresting him for vagrancy until we discovered he had over eight hundred dollars in his pocket."

I had received many such calls from all over the United States through the years: A phone call from a "Jesus Saves" rescue mission, as Dad called them; a concerned citizen that found him wandering aimlessly; an emergency room nurse; other police stations; VA hospitals; bus stations.

Even though I was used to getting the calls, they still frightened me, but I was always happy to know where he was when he disappeared. The policeman continued, "A known thief was wandering the park tonight. He could have easily beaten your dad up and robbed him. Actually, the officer picked him up before Wally got to him."

"Can I wire a bus ticket for him? What can I do?"

"He's not talking, except that he handed us this little card that has your information on it. The problem is, we don't know what to do with him. We don't want to turn him back into the cold."

"Thank you! Thank you so much for being kind to him!" By now I was crying and overwhelmed with gratitude that someone two thousand miles away was showing kindness to my dad. "He is a veteran. He has 100 percent VA benefits. He has a mental discharge from the army."

The officer seemed genuinely happy to be able to help Dad. "That's great! We'll take him to the VA hospital. They'll take care of him."

I couldn't go back to sleep. I continued to cry as I thought of my dad's life.

I reflected on the newspaper clipping he'd sent me a couple years before. It was a picture of him sleeping on a park bench, covered in snow with pigeons roosting on him. The caption said, "Man and pigeons share park bench in snowy Seattle."

I could imagine Dad reading *The Seattle Times* and seeing his picture there. He read the paper daily when he could get himself together enough to buy one or go to the library and read it. He had little to brag about to me, so I knew how proudly he sent me that picture of himself.

Mama, who had been struggling with sobriety for about two years, visited me in Sulphur. I had talked to her numerous times about my relationship with the Lord and had taken her to church with me occasionally. She really didn't understand how I could be so "religious."

But this particular visit she walked through The Son Shine Shop quietly, slowly looking at the many gifts and books. I had prayed daily that those coming in the shop would be inspired by what they saw. I had prayed there would be a resounding "Jesus loves you" radiating from all the items in our store.

I watched Mama tenderly touching the spines of devotional books that spoke of friendship with Jesus. I saw her reflecting on gifts that proclaimed in rainbow colors, "Do not be afraid. God loves you." But I wondered how much she actually understood.

I told her, "Mama, I want you to take home whatever you want. Take something for Aunt Daisy and your neighbors."

She hugged me. "Thank you, Pumpkin. Maybe I could take just a couple of things. You have some real pretty gifts here." I could tell she was proud of me, even if she didn't say it. Her mind was clearer now from no alcohol in her system.

I asked, "Will you come to church with me before you go back home to Hammond? I want to introduce you to Brother Sidney and my friends there." She seemed genuinely interested.

After church she packed up her suitcase and prepared to go home. She said, "I'm glad you're happy." It was part statement and part questioning of this new world of her daughter's. She had watched me devote my whole life to the experience I'd had at Northside Baptist Church that Sunday night.

She gathered up the treasures she had carefully picked out at the bookstore the day before. Once more she took them out of the bag to show me. There was a plaque that read, "God loves you so much He can't keep His eyes off of you!" She held it up. "I am going to put this in my kitchen window."

My heart seemed to burst with happiness. What did all this change mean? I'd prayed so much for her to have her own experience with God!

She pulled out a cup and saucer that said, "You are special to God." "Daisy's going to love this!" she exclaimed. Mama had many little items in her bag. She took them all out and looked at them in amazement. "I didn't even know there was anything like this."

I hugged her tight and said, "I love you so much Mama, and God loves you, too." She teared up but didn't say anything.

It seemed to me that she understood and saw me as a Christian for the first time. Through the years, many seeds had been sown in her heart, but I think the main seed that had taken root was watching the transformation that God had worked in my life. It was like the seed was beginning to sprout.

We talked about my relationship with God and the last twelve years since I had joined the church. Previously, she had never understood or comprehended the change in me, but this visit seemed to open her eyes in a new way. I understood God was mysteriously working in her life one touch at a time.

"Mama, do you remember when you used to come in my room and find me curled up on my bed reading those tracts and crying? I haven't changed much since then, huh?"

I could see the hurt and confusion in her eyes. I was sorry I had spoken of it.

She quickly said, "I'm glad those days are behind us."

I hugged her and then watched her as she drove away. My heart was full of love and concern for her.

A week later, she called me about seven o'clock in the morning saying, "My Jesus *awakened* me this morning at four o'clock, and I have been talking to Him ever since. Oh, Lana, I love Him so much!"

Jesus had actually woken her up? Amazing.

She loved him? Incredible.

She called Him "my Jesus"? A miracle.

From that day forth, she told everyone about her Jesus.

It was such an experience from darkness to light. She went from knowing nothing about God to wanting to know everything. Over the next several weeks, she had many questions. "Now Pumpkin, tell me who Mary is. That is Jesus' wife, isn't it?"

"No, Mama, Mary was Jesus' mother."

I brought her a Bible. She told me, "Pumpkin, thank you. I'm so excited to have it and to learn about my Jesus."

The next day she gave the Bible back. "I can't read this. You know how I hate snakes." She had read about the serpent tempting Eve in the Garden of Eden. She put it down and went no further.

Hmm, now what was I to do?

I gave her a large print Living Light devotional book. It was all scripture in an easy-to-understand translation. It is organized in a thought pattern. For example, for March 28, the subject is about God giving us strength. Every sentence is scripture arranged in a devotional style on strength and courage. She loved it!

She called and asked, "Is it OK to skip ahead and read? I keep reading today's over and over. I can't wait until tomorrow to read some more." It reminded me of how I read that box of tracts.

She called regularly with questions like, "I know who my Jesus is, but I'm reading about all these other names I really don't understand. Now, who is the Lord? Who is 'Son'? Who is 'Father'? How do they all fit in with my Jesus? Pumpkin, tell me the story again about when He was born. When the book talks about "Savior," that's my Jesus they are talking about, isn't it? I love Him so much!"

Mama called every day. "Daisy came over, and she was so angry with her neighbor. I gave her my *Living Light* to look at. I told her to turn to October 11. She read what my Jesus said about thinking on good things. I let her read the whole day." Mama's voice rang with excitement. "I think it helped her!"

She couldn't see me grinning on the other end of the phone. She read and quoted scriptures out of her *Living Light*, but her Bible references were days of the month.

She bubbled over to everyone, reminding me so much of myself twelve years before. She bought handkerchiefs for all her siblings to tuck in their pillowcases. She asked me to pray over them with her before she gave them out. She made sure she told them as I had told her, "It is not magic, but it is to remind you that God loves you and that me and Lana and Michael are praying for you!"

There was no question. Mama was *really* and *totally* sincere in her new life. We never talked about personal matters, so she never told me that she regretted the past. But after she died, her neighbor said, "Your mama sure did love you. She said she only wished she could go back and change things." I was shocked when he said that. It was the only indication I ever had that she was even aware of the trauma I had been put through.

CHAPTER
TWELVE

MICHAEL AND I DATED two years. He asked me over and over to marry him, but I kept saying, "No, not now." Michael had grown up in the Assembly of God church. He had uncles on both sides of his parents who were ministers. He was a "doesn't cuss, drink, or chew" kind of guy. I told him honestly, "Both of my parents have mental illnesses. I grew up around a barroom stool." I explained as much as I could, but he didn't really grasp the severity of their illnesses or what I was saying.

I did want to be married. I felt that Michael was the most spiritual person I had ever known. I knew I would never find anyone more committed to the Lord than he was. We were both thirty, and neither of us had been married before.

One Sunday morning as Michael and I were driving away from the church, I said, "I have something I want to tell you."

"OK, what is it?"

"I want to marry you."

He slammed on his brakes in the middle of the road. I think he had just about given up hope. "You what?"

"I want to marry you."

Michael pulled to the side of the road. He hugged me and kept saying over and over, "Thank you, Lord. Thank you, Lord."

After getting to know both of my parents, Michael felt at a loss in trying to have any kind of relationship with either of them. "Lana, I only tell you this as a fact, not because I want to hurt you. There are saner people locked away in the mental hospitals than your parents, who are walking the street!"

I had to laugh. I knew he was right. But this was the only life I had known with either of them. They seemed almost normal to me.

Michael and I set a date for our wedding. We began to build a home and planned to get married and move in. We were putting all our resources into the construction, and it was pretty obvious that we could save money by not having a big wedding. Besides, we both looked on crowds with dread. Neither one of us liked the limelight or for anyone to focus on us. Michael more than enthusiastically agreed when I suggested, "Let's have a private wedding with just witnesses."

I told Judy our plans. "No, you can't do that," she told me. "You have to have a wedding for us to all come to!"

I explained, "I don't want to draw attention to myself. I feel like people would come to our wedding out of obligation. I don't want to inconvenience anyone."

Judy shook her head. "Lana, people look up to you. You have been a respected business leader in the community for two years. The Son Shine Shop has been a lighthouse to many people. The women in Women's Aglow love and admire you. Please don't think of your wedding as an inconvenience to your friends."

One of the other board members, Kay, insisted on giving me a shower. "Now, Lana, I want you to go down to the China Closet and register for china and silverware."

I told Michael, "I feel like I'm being rude not to go along with what they want to do for us. How can I say no when they are so gracious?"

I survived the shower because I was surrounded by such kind ladies, who had given lots of effort and time. About sixty-five ladies attended! I never said, "Oh wow! This is so awesome," but I tried to show everyone how grateful I was for their friendship.

With Kay's help, I planned a simple wedding around the Lord. I had originally bought an inexpensive, knee-length white dress to wear. Kay took one look at it and said, "Lana, that will not do. You need a full-length wedding dress."

I took my dress to Reesa, an accomplished seamstress. "Is there anything that can be done with this dress to make it floor-length and more wedding-y?"

She laughed. "Yes, I think I can do that."

My Aglow friends worked with me on the details. It was a simple wedding but exactly right for Michael and me.

For the wedding, Mama wore a blue chiffon dress. She looked beautiful and happy as she stood in the back of the church waiting to be escorted down the aisle by Michael's cousin, Kenneth. She was the only family I had there. I overheard her saying, "You know, my daughter owns a bookstore. She has such wonderful things in there about Jesus." All I could do was hug her tightly. There had been such a dramatic change in her life the previous few months.

"Mama, I love you so much!" I told her.

"Pumpkin, I love you, and I love Michael too. I am so proud of you!" She said it wholeheartedly.

Brother Sidney gave me away. He and his wife had always lovingly supported me and stepped in when I needed them. Of course, I wanted my dad at my side, but I knew he was completely unable to be with a festive crowd, much less to have people focusing on him.

The church was full. My friend, Beth, played the organ as I entered to "Bless the Lord All My Soul." Michael was waiting at the front of the church in a new brown suit that we had gone shopping for. He was beaming.

I carried a single red long-stemmed rose. It seemed surreal as I looked into people's faces as I walked down the aisle. My Aglow friends who I looked up to smiled lovingly at me.

There was Bitsy, the lady who had welcomed me the first day I opened the bookstore. There was Catherine, who would become much, much more than a friend. I nodded to Delores, Brother Sidney's wife. There was Michael's uncle and his family, including Clara, who had been the manager of Good News Book Store.

As we walked from the church after the ceremony, Beth played "For He Has Done Great Things."

I was bursting with happiness. *Yes, God, You, indeed, have done great things.*

It was Mother's Day. Mama came out to meet me at my car when I drove up. "Pumpkin, I fixed shrimp gumbo for you."

"Mama, take my suitcase. I have a gift for you that is too heavy for you to carry." Michael and I had bought her a microwave. Michael had a good job at a chemical plant, and he wanted to make sure Mama was taken care of.

Mama and I spent our time watching, *I Love Lucy* on TV and eating gumbo. She shared with me from her *Living Light*.

The day before I left, I went and got us each a shrimp po' boy to go. Mama was still tormented by her phobias. I sat on the couch to watch TV and eat my sandwich. Mama ate at the small table in the kitchen. "Pumpkin, come and taste my sandwich and see if it's like yours." This was what we had gone through for so many, many years. I obediently got up and went to her.

She tore off a small piece of her sandwich and watched me eat it. She then tore off another piece from another section and intently watched me eat that piece also. "Yeah, Mama, it tastes good." My heart felt broken because she was in so much misery, always fearing someone, fearing that even her Pumpkin was poisoning her.

I didn't know her torment was getting ready to end forever.

Before I left, I took her mother-looking handkerchief out of her pillowcase and prayed, "Lord, we pray for peace. As Mama lies her head on her pillow each night, let her pillow be her special, quiet meeting place between You and her as she goes to sleep at night. I ask that You would continue to be her constant companion. Hug her in Your love. Amen."

Mama was smiling when I looked up. "That is just what He does, Lana. He hugs me in His love! I read my scripture readings during the day, but I always read them before I go to bed at night. I lay my head on my pillow with all the prayers that you pray for me. And I feel like my Jesus is hugging me all through the night."

Mama walked me out to the car when I left. "I love you with all my heart, Mama!" I told her.

"I love you a big bunch, Pumpkin!"

We kept waving and blowing kisses at each other until I could no longer see her with my eyes. I could definitely see her in my heart!

One week later, I was waiting for the bricklayer to arrive. He was putting brick on the addition that Michael and I made to our house. We had added a full efficiency apartment in hopes that Mama or Dad might come and live with us. The phone rang at eight o'clock in the morning. My aunt's husband hollered on the other end, "Get over here right now! Your mother's dead!"

I couldn't comprehend what he was saying.

"Your aunt and I came over to your mama's because she wouldn't answer her phone last night. We came early this morning, and she wouldn't answer the door. We broke the door down and found her dead in her bed!"

Aunt Daisy's daughter, Jo Ann, got on the phone. "Lana, are you OK?"

I was in a state of disbelief. "Jo, you know sometimes you think people have died and really they haven't? Please go shake her for me. Try Jo, please. Do it for me. Shake her real hard!"

"Honey, they're taking your mama out in the hearse now. Dr. Forest is here."

Dr. Forest was Mama's doctor. Jo gave him the phone. He gently said, "Lana, your mother died of a massive heart attack. You know she had a grossly enlarged and diseased heart."

"Yes, I know." My voice sounded little and faraway.

He and I had talked before about Mama's heart condition. He had told me that the many years of alcohol abuse had severely damaged her heart, and it was finally catching up with her.

I called Michael at the plant. He couldn't get to the house until a relief came in for him. It seemed like I had to wait forever. Finally, he picked me up and we drove the 175 miles to Hammond with flashers on the whole distance.

I sobbed, and Michael tried to comfort me, "Your mama has it made now. She's in heaven for all eternity. She's finally at peace. Don't you know she's having a great time with her Jesus?"

I couldn't say anything. I was too stunned, and I couldn't stop sobbing.

My mind went to my visit with Judy Robinson a few days before. I had walked into Judy's house. "Hey, I'm here," I announced.

Judy had responded, "Hey, I'll be right there. How was your visit with your mother?"

"It was great. We had a really good time." Then I told her something that had seemed a little odd. "While I was there, I dreamed that she died. It was so real. I went in and shook her awake to make sure she was alive. Later that day, I felt the Lord gave me this scripture verse and it was about Mama.

> When our human bodies die and are transformed into bodies that will never die, then will this scripture be fulfilled. Death is swallowed up in victory. O death where is your sting? O grave where is your victory?
>
> —1 CORINTHIANS 15:53–54

I told Judy, "I wrote it in my journal, but I didn't want to hear that."

She hugged me, "I'm sure you didn't." We both ignored it.

Now, speeding to Hammond, I wondered why I had not been more alert. I should have been there when she died. I should have paid attention to that dream. I reached in the back seat and retrieved my journal. I could only see it sporadically through my blinding tears. I opened it to my notes from the previous night. I had written this:

> We appreciate the Light the most when it is dark. His grace is sufficient.

Then right there on Interstate 10, I clearly heard the voiceless voice of God say, "If you had understood she was dying, you would have been with her. She would have been clinging to you. I reserved her home-going special for her and Me. My grace was sufficient for her. She let me hold her and lead her into eternity!"

Michael drove straight to the funeral home. Jo Ann was in the office waiting for me. I hugged her and said. "I want to see my mother."

A man in a stiff dark suit intoned, "The body is not prepared yet."

"I don't care; I want to see my mother."

We walked into the casket room, and her body was wheeled out on a stretcher. She was wrapped in a white sheet with her head exposed. I ran my fingers over her forehead and her cheeks. *Oh, Mama I wish you knew how much I loved you.* I laid my head on her chest and wept. I stayed with her as long as they would let me.

Before I left Sulphur, Jo Ann had asked me on the phone, "What do you want to dress her in?"

"The dress she wore at my wedding."

Jo Ann called back to say, "I can't find it. Shall I go buy her something?"

"Buy an orchid dress."

"OK. Lana, the funeral home wants to know how to fix her hair."

"No wig. I want her to look natural."

At Mama's house, Aunt Daisy, slightly plump and graying, put her arms around me and comforted me as she had so many years ago. "Your mama would be proud to see us together. She would be real happy."

Michael and I went back to the funeral home at two o'clock. Mama's hair was all teased and in a ridiculous bouffant. I ran my hand through her hair over and over to take the tease out. I desperately wanted her to look natural, to have the mother look.

Michael looked down on her. "I'm proud to be her son-in-law. We could all learn from her childlike faith in God." He kissed me and said, "I'm going to leave you alone with her for a while."

I fastened Mama's favorite pin to her dress. It was a red, heart-shaped pin that declared "Jesus Loves Me." I sobbed some more and again laid my head on her chest and hugged her. I had never had anyone close to me die. Actually, besides Michael I really never had anyone close to me except Mama.

Brother Sidney and Michael, who is a lay minister, spoke at Mama's funeral. Michael read some of the many scriptures that Mama had underlined in her worn-out *Living Light.*

Michael had a completely opposite background than Mama and I had. He was raised on a church pew by a praying mother. But that day, Mama was celebrated as the one who knew God in a powerful way! My husband, whom I respect as one of the spiritual giants in my life, wept as he said, "Someday I hope to know God the way Lana's mother knew God!"

Mama died at age fifty-eight, three years after she became a Christian. She showed everyone the miraculous power of God. How one touch from Him is greater than all the world can offer!

CHAPTER
THIRTEEN

OVER ONE HUNDRED AND fifty ladies crowded into that first Aglow meeting in Sulphur. It was dismaying to find out that as an officer I had to sit at the head table. When I pulled out my chair and sat down, it seemed all seventy ladies stared at me. I knew they were thinking, *What is she doing up there? She doesn't belong.*

I had carefully selected a tan skirt and a dressy white blouse. Usually I didn't really wear jewelry or makeup, but for that day I bought a necklace to match my outfit. I didn't want my fellow leaders to be embarrassed by my plain-Jane appearance. Still, I felt like I looked like little orphan Annie.

Judy had asked me to make the announcements. I sat there trying to look as casual as the other officers, but my stomach jiggled like the Jell-O salad that was on the buffet. When I looked at the agenda Judy had set out at each of the officer's places, I realized it was my turn. I walked to the microphone with my heart in my throat. If she'd asked me to say a prayer, I could have done it easily. But announcements?

When Judy handed out our assignments the night before, I'd prayed and prayed over my small part in the meeting. *Lord, You know I can't face all those people. I don't belong there. I'm the little barroom girl among roses. Lord, I know everything in the announcements are important, so I ask that You would make the announcements through me.*

I got through them and went back to my seat. I hadn't messed up or forgotten anything. I hadn't tripped. *Oh, Lord, thank You.*

Driving home from the meeting, I continued to pray for all who had attended the meeting. *Lord, please meet each one at their point of need. Give them peace and heal their heartaches.*

I didn't pray about the negative thoughts that hounded me at every turn. My own heartaches from my past were buried so deeply, I didn't even know they were there. I never challenged my harsh judgment against myself. I had a made-up my mind that I was inadequate as a human being. I thought the facts were the facts.

For over a year I watched Judy introduce the speakers and lead the board meetings. She made everyone feel welcome; she chatted with our guests, advisors, and strangers. She could sit down at a table and talk to everyone at once. Judy belonged there. I was amazed as I watched her warmly interact with everyone.

I didn't belong. I was scared to open my mouth. I never had anything to contribute to any of the social conversations. I had no stories that I would want anyone to hear about my family or growing up. I was overwhelmed at the thought of having to chat about normal life experiences.

The place I was most happy and at peace was in my bookstore. One morning I helped a gentleman find the perfect gift for his wife, whom he said was depressed. I quietly prayed that God would lead me to the right book or gift that would transform her life. I genuinely believed everything in our shop had the potential to bring people hope and minister to their needs.

"This is a leatherette daily devotional book that I could imprint her name on and gift wrap at no charge." I showed him some elegant wall décor that had an encouraging scripture at the bottom of the print.

"I like the idea of inspirational thoughts every day," he said. "I'll take the devotional book." I gave him a piece of paper to write his wife's name on.

I looked at the name he wrote down. "Lenda." I smiled at him. "That's an unusual spelling. Is this how she spells it? With an *e*?"

He looked at it again. "Oh no, it's not! Thanks for noticing that."

We laughed together. I loved the bookstore and all the people who came in. I knew God used me to put just the right items in their hands. I handed him his package. "God bless you."

Just then the phone rang. It was Judy. "Lana, the selection committee feels like you're to take my place as the new Aglow president." Judy knew me well enough to know that this was the last thing I expected or wanted. "Please don't say no, Lana. I too, believe you are God's choice. He has been preparing you for over a year now."

I leaned against the counter, almost weak. How could I ever do all the things that Judy did? But how could I say no to God? "I don't think I can do this, Judy, but I'll pray about it."

As I prayed, I knew this was something God wanted me to do. So, willing and scared at the same time, I agreed.

Over the years I'd become resourceful in coping with awkward situations and trying to divert attention away from myself. As the new Aglow president, I dealt with my insecurities by assigning the other officers the leadership responsibilities for opening and closing the meeting.

After my second meeting as president, Judy and Margie approached me with serious expressions. "Lana, can we talk with you?" We three sat alone in the cavernous Chateau Charles. Judy began, "The meetings are going great, Lana, but you need to open them. You're assigning your officers all the leadership roles you need to take."

Margie continued, "You're the president. The group looks up to you. They need to see you take charge."

As Judy and Margie then began to compliment me, my mind drifted. I slipped away from the conversation. I imagined myself standing outside in the cold alone, peeking through the window at this gathering. Everyone inside was warm, laughing, enjoying each other's company, sharing the week's events.

Judy and Margie were still pointing out my good qualities, so I continued to zone out. I saw myself shivering in the cold. I began to wallow in my self-talk. *Why would anyone want me to come in? I didn't fit there. I didn't belong. They'd disapprove if I intruded on them.*

I realized Judy and Margie had stopped talking. I sheepishly said, "OK, I will open the meetings. You are right. You're right. I'll begin to show more authority."

Driving home from the meeting that day, I passionately prayed for God to minister to the needs of those who had attended our meeting. "Heal their broken hearts, give them peace." Again, I didn't ask God to heal me from my own wounds. I thought all of that was in my past. I couldn't see how entrenched I was in my negative self-talk. I was convinced I was different, and I defiantly refused to believe anything else.

After my term of office was up as local president, I was asked to serve on the area board. There were only two area boards in the state of Louisiana, so we had oversight over a large part of the state. I was only comfortable in my position as leadership training coordinator because Judy was at the helm as area president.

Judy and I spent lots of time together. She had many friends, but for me it was pretty much all business. I loved and admired her as the multitude of others did, but I certainly would never imagine she considered me a close friend. If we were not talking about God or preparing for a meeting, I felt like a bump on a log. I didn't know what to say, how to act, or even how to blend in.

Then it was too late. Judy's husband was transferred to Arkansas. I was selected to take Judy's position as area president. As Judy was hugging me good-bye, she said, "I know you feel abandoned. If I were to select a new close friend for you, it would be Margie."

All I could think was, *Me? Why did she use the term close friend in relation to me? I'm not the kind of person who has close friends.*

I saw Judy and Margie as two women who were immensely loved and admired by everyone who knew them. They both were sought-after speakers. Even though we were friends, I was still intimidated by both of them. If I was in any setting with either of them, all the attention and adoring eyes were on them. It fed into my "I don't fit, I don't belong" self-talk.

I had been asked to speak at an Aglow Meeting in DeRidder, Louisiana, and tell about my life. At the end of the meeting, most of the women came forward for personal prayer.

They told me things like, "The Lord really used you tonight," and, "What an awesome testimony." And on and on the people hugged me and thanked me for coming. But as we walked out the door, my friend Ann said, "Lana that was good, but you didn't talk about yourself. You talked about your mother."

Lord, I don't know who I am apart from Mama. I don't know why I accepted the position as area president. At the time I thought You wanted me to. All of the officers on the board with me can run circles around me in every way. I'm scared. I think I'm in over my head.

Yet, there were some places where I was totally at home.

"Lana, would you like to come with my team to a service we conduct at a nursing home?" The man asking was a lay minister who often came into the bookstore.

"I might be. How often do you meet?"

"Weekly."

When I got there, I was in my element—a multitude of people with needs and me, who wanted to help those with needs!

I started going back to the nursing home on my own. I went from room to room asking, "How are you today? Can I get something for you?" I smiled, hugged, and simply said, "God bless you." At first I went once a week, then twice a week, then almost every day.

I felt bad for the people who were stuck there. I gravitated to several disabled middle-aged ladies, Frances, Liz, Thelma, Muriel, and Irene. They didn't seem to have any visitors, and I hated for anyone to feel sad or lonely. I kidded around with them and talked about what was going on in the small world of the nursing home. When they complained about the food, I started bringing hamburgers and fried chicken. When the others had gone to bed, we sat in the big lobby, chatted, and ate.

I started taking some of these new friends to the Aglow meeting. I solicited help from others, and we picked them up once a month. Sometimes I filled up my car and brought them to my house for lunch. I was having fun, and I thought they were, too. That was the whole point, to help relieve their loneliness and boredom.

Our Aglow retreat was coming up. I thought it would be great to take several women from the home on retreat. I could pay their way and look after them, even though I had tons of other responsibilities.

While visiting with my friend, Janette, I shared all the difficult logistics I had to figure out in order to accomplish this. Janette's daughter, Connie, had Down syndrome. I thought Janette would be empathetic to my dilemma and pleased I was going to all the trouble. One thing I liked about my friend Janette was I could depend on her to be direct. I never had to wonder what she was thinking.

In her normal fashion, she stated what was on her mind. "Lana, have you ever thought that what you're doing for those ladies is not really good for them? They're secure in the setting they're in. Taking them out of their setting can be scary for them." Her tone was firm. "You may be happy, but they may not be."

I was totally surprised. "No, I never thought of it. I guess I really never considered their point of view. I thought I knew what they needed."

"Lana, if you would back away and look at it and talk to them about it, I think you'll see things differently."

The rest of that day, I reflected on how I'd assumed I knew what they needed. When I offered my services, I hadn't really listened to any objections; I'd never considered the possibility that they may not want my help.

I went back to the nursing home and began listening. I found out most of the time the women were happy to just have me come and visit. Yes, sometimes it was stressful for them to have to load up and leave the home.

I was learning, but I wondered about other times when I'd put on my taking-care-of-Mama hat and rescued people who did not want to be rescued.

Meanwhile, the area board was responsible for conducting retreats for the local chapters to attend. Margie and I and our other three officers made plans for a retreat at Toro Hills, a beautiful resort area in Many, Louisiana. We agreed to invite Judy Robinson to speak for an afternoon session. We knew everyone would be excited to see her again.

I couldn't help feeling anxious about the retreat. Margie was on the board, and now Judy was speaking. Even though I was area president, I always felt substandard when I was with those two dynamic women. My negative self-talk bounced off the walls.

I thought Margie would be a much better person than I to oversee the afternoon session. I told her, "I need you to oversee the meeting. You can get whomever you like to help you."

Margie looked at me surprised. "Where are you going to be?"

"Oh, I'll be around, but I'd like for you to be in charge."

After the meeting ended, Judy almost reprimanded me. "What happened to the meeting, Lana? I had the most difficult time speaking. Margie did a good job in her part, but there was something spiritually wrong. I felt like I was fighting a battle. I'm going to go back to the room and pray. I think you should get with your board and pray, too. We need to get straight whatever is beginning to hinder the meetings."

I got alone with God that afternoon. *Dear God, what went wrong? I know Judy is right, that the meeting was a struggle.* As I waited, I heard clearly that voiceless voice of God: "You abdicated your authority over the meeting to Margie."

I began to understand. I was the one God had chosen as president to oversee the retreat, and I had given the job of leadership away. I could have delegated the authority, but I was not to not abdicate or renounce my authority. God had not called Margie to be president. He had called me, and I was to lead whether I felt secure or insecure. It had nothing to do with whom could do a better job. It was about whom God wanted to do the work.

And so, that afternoon I discovered an important spiritual principle: I cannot put off my God-given responsibilities on others. They were not spiritually equipped if God had not called them to do it. I had given the job of leadership away when it was not for me to give.

I went to Margie and apologized for throwing the meeting in her lap. Before the evening meeting, I went to Judy's room. "I know what happened. I didn't rise to the occasion as the retreat leader."

Judy looked over at her mother, Selma, who had come from Texas to attend the retreat. Judy told her mother, "Tell Lana what you told me."

Selma was one of my favorite people. She had the "mother look." She warmly smiled at me. "Judy was upset after her meeting and was questioning what had happened. I told her, 'Lana is intimidated by Margie and has turned the retreat over to her.'"

Back in my room, I realized my extreme insecurities had actually caused me to be disobedient to God. *Lord,* I prayed, *forgive me for not trusting You to accomplish what You've asked me to do.*

I continued to try to rescue my dad. At one point, I owned three places at the same time for him to live. In my co-dependent mind, I thought, *When he gets paranoid about his neighbors, he can go to one of his other homes.* That way he would be within my reach rather than disappearing across the country somewhere. Of course, that didn't always work.

The main home I had for him was a fourteen-foot-wide trailer settled on a large piece of property. At his request, I put a padlocked chain link fence around it. I kept the utilities on and stocked it with food. When he left, I never knew if he would ever come back or if he would be gone days or months. But he kept returning; it was the only security he had.

I also bought a small, two-bedroom brick home across town that he could stay in part time if he felt the need to flee. He only spent one night there.

I knew no limits when it came to the needs of either of my parents. I didn't know why I made so many irrational choices concerning them. It was just that they were my parents and I loved them dearly!

I told my dad regularly how much I loved him and how proud I was of him. "You're the smartest man I know." That was true. He was well read on a vast range of subjects. "You know much more of the Bible than I do." That was also true. He had in his possession, most of the time, some type of religious literature. I'd given him books and a small Bible with his name imprinted on it. When his duffle bag was lost or stolen, he often trotted off to find more Christian reading material. I don't know how many times I'd replaced his Bible.

I was proud of his military record. He was a captain in WWII and fought in some of the major battles. He led troops onto Omaha Beach in the battle of Normandy. I had read many accounts of the tragedies of WWII, and my dad fit the description of the men who "never came home from the war." Dad often had delusions of snipers behind buildings. He rambled about the Green Berets and Hitler.

One day after church I went over to his trailer to check on everything. I often did that. He had been gone about two weeks this time. He usually cleaned the trailer out when he left town. If I had the good fortune of seeing him before he left, he often told me, "I won't ever come back, so I'm leaving nothing behind." He always stripped the walls bare; he thought the pictures on the wall were talking to him.

I drove up the driveway to the fence. I saw the front door was open. *He's home!* That was a nice surprise. I never walked in on him unexpected, so I called. "Dad, Dad, it's Susan." I climbed the steps. He was lying on the floor.

He was dead.

He had come home to die.

Michael and I and many friends prayed often that he would be here with me if he died. I didn't want him to be lost somewhere and me not know what happened to him.

I found out from a taxi driver that he had come home the night before. He must have known he was dying, because he uncharacteristically had his money laid out on a table, as if to leave it for his daughter to find. The other thing he did, I believe, said it all. He had taped up on the wall a tract. It had a cross on it, and it said, "Jesus Saves!"

Thank you, Lord, for reminding me that Your love knows no limit. In my dad's limitations, You were limitless. Thank You for having him put that tract on the wall just for me to assure me that, indeed, He is safe with You now for all eternity!

As Aglow president, our board and I made special preparations for Pat Robertson's wife, DeDe, to speak at our Sulphur meeting. Even though the room was packed, I was not outwardly intimidated by having a big-name speaker. By then I had become skilled in my defense mechanisms, so skilled I could usually control my responses to social dilemmas.

It was important that I kept that control and did not let my guard down. Letting it down would mean I would have major difficulty functioning.

I'd never entertained any thoughts of the possibility that I was of any value. It was painful for me to reflect on anything positive concerning myself. As a child and a teenager I recited often, "I am a non-person." After committing my life to God, I had continued to reinforce that.

I hammered myself with, "He is all, and I am nothing!" True but also untrue. He certainly did not see me as nothing. He saw me as valuable enough to die for.

I didn't know I had an alternative. It didn't even occur to me to ask God to change my way of thinking. I didn't even look for an escape.

CHAPTER

FOURTEEN

MICHAEL INSISTED, "LANA YOU really need to go see Dr. Thibodeaux about your severe headaches."

They had been going on for a year, so I promised him, "When I finish with my Aglow presidency next month, I'll go to the doctor." I had been local president, area president, and now was serving once more as the local president.

Finally, I made the appointment, and the doctor began ordering tests.

In the meantime, my friend, Paula, came into the bookstore to browse. She mentioned, "I've been taking medication to control my schizophrenia."

My ears perked up. "My dad was paranoid schizophrenic, but he never was able to take medication because of his alcoholism."

Paula invited me, "Why don't you come with me to the NAMI support group tonight? It stands for National Alliance on Mental Illness. Usually just my parents go, but tonight is an informational meeting and we're going as a family. They meet weekly to discuss the far-reaching effects of mental illness. Let's go together."

It sounded like a way to learn more about my dad's illness. "Yes, I'd very much like to go. I've never talked to anyone about my dad's schizophrenia."

There were about twelve of us, ranging from a teenager to an elderly woman, at the mental health clinic. We sat in a large circle. Immediately, I began to feel uncomfortable.

The facilitator talked for about ten minutes and then said, "We'll go around the circle, give our names, and tell a little about our situation. You can pass if you don't want to talk."

I had no idea why, but I began to shake. I was doing all I could do to keep from bursting out crying. When it came to my turn, I said, "My name's Lana. Pass." I really don't know much of what happened at that meeting. I trembled the whole time.

After the meeting was over, Paula and I went to get pizza. I cried while I ate. I blubbered some things that I was sure were incoherent to her because they were certainly incoherent to me.

When I dropped Paula at her home, she asked, "Lana, do you think you'll start going to the support group?" I was so disoriented from my first encounter with them that I was sure I would not go back. I mumbled something about being so busy.

As soon as I backed out of her driveway, I began uncontrollably crying and shaking. Then I began praying out loud, as I usually did when I was alone. *Lord, what's going on? Obviously, something's the matter. I don't know what's happening. Help me work through this. I want everything You have to give me. I don't want to stop short of getting Your best. You know my heart is open to You to work through this. Help me!*

During the next couple of weeks, I kept questioning the Lord about my traumatic experience at the support group. *Lord, what happened at that meeting? It totally rattled my cage. All I can say is, "Help me understand."*

By the time I got to Dr. Thibodeaux's office, I was more than a little anxious. I didn't think there was anything serious, but the chronic headaches were becoming more severe.

Dr. Thibodeaux began, "The feeling of your head being in a vice-grip is classic for migraine and tension headaches. Since your tests don't show any physical problems, I think maybe stress is causing your symptoms. Are you under a lot of stress?"

Hmmm. That was an easy question to answer. "No."

"Tell me a little bit about yourself."

I told her about the bookstore, my work in Aglow, and speaking regularly at various meetings and retreats. "But, I love it all. I don't feel stressed or pressured by my schedule. I'm used to being busy."

Dr. Thibodeaux responded, "Tell me about how you grew up. I think the problem is deeper than your current activities."

I thought that was a strange thing to say, but by then I had a little canned speech that I gave when anyone asked me about my past. So with no emotion, I began, "Both of my parents were alcoholics and mentally ill. I am an only child. My mom married several times. We had a role-reversal. She was unable to mother me, so I mothered her. I became a Christian when I was a senior in high school, and I've been active in the church ever since."

That was it. My life was summed up in an emotionless fifteen seconds! And I had fought for years to keep it that way.

I couldn't read the look on her face as she stared at me. I began to feel very uncomfortable. Then in an almost inaudible voice, she gently said, "I believe when you joined the church you slammed the door on a mountain of pain. Because you haven't dealt with your pain, the stress of it is literally eating away at your body." She kept talking, "You said you have had bad headaches for most of your life but for over a year now they've been increasing in severity and frequency. Is that right?"

I was beginning to blank out and dissociate from the conversation. I fought hard to keep my composure. I simply answered, "Yes."

She sensed I was spacing out on her. "Lana, pay attention to what I'm saying. Even at your young age of thirty-nine, you can have very serious health issues from being wrapped so tight." She stopped and looked closely at me. "Have you ever been to counseling?"

I needed something to hold on to! The room was spinning. Blood was pounding in my ears.

I simply said, "No." I didn't tell her that I didn't believe I needed counseling.

Through my leadership in Aglow, I had become good friends with many people who spoke on emotional healing. I carried many books in the bookstore on the subject as well. Personally, I didn't believe it was for me. I didn't think I was in denial. I just honestly had never considered it for me. I was happy with my relationship with God, and the past was the past.

Dr. Thibodeaux informed me, "I'm going to make an appointment for you." I think she sensed I wouldn't follow through with it for myself.

I had a long drive home and plenty of time to reflect on what had just happened. What did she mean by me being "wrapped so tight"?

I knew I was generally super-responsible and hyper-vigilant. I liked being in control of situations. I knew I didn't risk being spontaneous, letting my guard down, or opening up to people. I laughed. *Lord, maybe that's being wrapped tight.*

Dr. Thibodeaux's nurse called me back that afternoon. "Your appointment is with Rose. The doctor thinks you may need long-term counseling."

I tried to put it all out of my mind. I was pretty good at doing that. I didn't even know what to pray. I was confused about my reactions to the brief support group experience and my doctor's visit, but I felt obligated to go to at least one of the counseling sessions.

I explained to Michael, "The doctor thinks I need counseling."

He looked alarmed. "Does it have to do with our marriage? I told you I didn't know how to deal with your parents, and I don't think I can deal with my wife having emotional problems."

"No, it's not about our marriage. It's just that I'm feeling some confusion."

"Please talk to anyone you want. I think—I think this is good."

A week later, I walked into Rose's office. I had absolutely no idea what to expect. She asked me to talk to her about my visit with Dr. Thibodeaux. I went through my canned story and the doctor's comments about it.

I prayed, *Lord, I don't want to get involved in a bunch of psychological mumbo jumbo. You are all I need. Please protect me.*

Rose asked, "How did that make you feel not having your mother emotionally present for you?"

I immediately blanked out. I couldn't think of one thing to say. I sat frozen to my chair.

After it was obvious I wasn't going to say anything, Rose said an odd thing. "Breathe."

I stared at her. Rose was short with blondish, white hair. I sat only a few feet from her in her small office. There must have been pictures or certificates on the wall, but I didn't see them. Still unable to speak, I questioned her with my eyes.

"You need to breathe. You're holding all your feelings in with such a vengeance that you're holding your breath." She continued, "Put words to what you're thinking right now. Let your mouth voice your feelings. If you have never talked about the trauma you experienced as a child, you need to talk about it."

I was beginning to feel embarrassed. I didn't want to be rude or stubborn. I just didn't know what to say. My past was in my past. I didn't have anything to talk about.

Rose prodded again, "Please talk to me. Tell me what is going on in your head right now."

"I don't feel like I have anything to talk about. I don't live in the past. I feel like I'm OK."

"OK, let's do it this way then. Tell me about your mother. What kind of things did you do together? Where did you live? Start at the beginning. We're not in a hurry. I really do want to hear about your life."

I felt like I could talk about my mama. "Actually, I would love to brag on her. I adored her. It's been six years since she died, and I still miss her." I selectively left out the bad parts. "She was beautiful. She was married several times and had lots of boyfriends. I am the only child either of my parents had. I couldn't have loved them any more if they had both been perfect."

Rose finally found a vulnerable part she thought she could explore. "Let's talk about the parts that weren't perfect about them."

Once again, I found myself praying, *Lord, I don't know where all this is going. All I can say is, "Please protect me."*

I began to ramble about the bars, the drinking, the mental illness, and the men.

"Breathe, Lana."

I took a breath.

"What were you doing in the midst of all this? I want to talk about you."

I felt paralyzed. I was blank. My hands were profusely perspiring. Rose said, "Put words to what is going on with you right now." "I'm blank. I do this often." "Tell me about times when you do this." After another very long silence, I said, "My mind is blank. I can't think of anything to say. I feel like I'm going to throw up!" "OK, let's quit for today. Are you willing to come back? If you don't know how to answer, let me say this as gently as I know how: you do need to come back weekly." She gave me an assignment. "I want you to write down what happened today. If you don't know what to say, then write, 'I went blank.' Try to add more words to every thought you experienced while we were together this hour."

I had an hour's drive home. *Lord, the one thing I know is I want to do your will. I'm so confused. Something is wrong, and I don't know what it is.*

One of the questions Rose asked kept rolling over in my head: "Do you remember the first time you experienced this extreme anxiety to the point of blanking out?" The more I tried to reflect back to when I began blanking out, the more I blanked out.

Lord, I need you right in the middle of what I'm going through. I want everything You have to offer. Obviously, something is the matter. All I can do is trust that You are the one that rocked my boat, beginning when I went to that NAMI meeting a few weeks ago.

The next couple of sessions with Rose went pretty much the same. I felt like a zombie staring at her most of the time. It was like my brain simply shut down, like a deer caught in headlights. I didn't know what to say.

Each week Rose repeated, "Don't reject what I'm saying. Just put it on a shelf to look at during the week. This is the first time you've had a reality check. The process has started. Let's not stop."

After about a month, I began feeling more comfortable with her. She asked me, "What is your self-talk? Some people say, 'I'm stupid,' or 'I'm fat,' or 'I'm a failure,' or 'I'm ugly'. What is it that you say to yourself over and over again that is keeping you stuck?"

Stuck? I had never thought of myself as stuck. "What do you mean I'm stuck?"

"You have said that you often shut down in social settings, that you avoid crowds unless you're in a leadership role, that you stop dead in your tracks when someone inquires about your family of origin. I would say that hinders you in the real world called life. What do you think?"

"I don't belong in the real world." That was the matter of fact statement that I believed. I had never said it out loud.

"Explain what you mean by that."

"I feel like a little barroom girl that is out of place everywhere in real life. I love God with all my heart, and I feel like I have a place with Him. Other than that, I don't fit. I don't belong. I am a non-person."

"Lana, those are all deductions you came to believe when you were a child. You're a successful adult woman now. It's time for you to begin enjoying life." She continued, "Those statements are not true. They are lies that you made up in your mind."

I was reeling as Rose kept on talking. "As a child you felt pushed away over and over again. You couldn't find a home for your heart, so you came to the erroneous conclusion that you didn't fit and you didn't belong anywhere."

I began to sob. The last time I had uncontrollably sobbed was when my mama died.

Rose began to prod, "Please put words to your emotions. What are you thinking?" She had to keep repeating, "Open your mouth. Say what you're feeling."

Finally, I blurted out the whole reason for my pain: "I wanted my mother!"

CHAPTER
FIFTEEN

Rose REPEATED SOFTLY, "You wanted your mother."

"I had no one! I know she was sick and couldn't be there for me. But I had this all-consuming yearning for her to take care of me. I know this sounds stupid, but somehow that feeling has never left me!"

I continued to sob. "I feel like I live in absolute confusion of this conflict. On one hand I have this yearning deep inside. And then as quick as the feeling rises, I slam it down. It's too painful to even think about."

Rose handed me the box of tissue. While I was trying to gain my composure, she talked. "A young child depends on adults. That is a fact of life. From your birth, your mother and father were locked in conflict and mental illness. After their divorce, your mother was grasping for her own survival. On every hand you were neglected. You literally had no stability or anything you could depend on."

I could feel myself fading from her. She said, "OK, focus Lana. You are in there hiding somewhere. You're in a safe place here. We're making a breakthrough here. Let's keep on looking at the truth. Try to open your heart and listen. I have no reason to lie to you."

I was in a daze, but I struggled to listen.

She continued, "It wasn't like things were good and then they got bad. You had no way of knowing what healthy behavior was. You had nothing to compare your life to. Lana, I want to encourage you to begin to read books of others who grew up in dysfunctional homes, go to support groups, keep talking, and keep listening. There are other people who would like to share their story with you and would also like to hear yours. It's also time for you to start sharing with your close friends."

Rose kept talking. "Very early in your development, you put on a cast iron emotional suit! As a child, that was your survival. As an adult, it's not working."

Driving home that day, the sun shone brightly through the car window, like the light that Rose had begun to shine on my past. *Lord, You know I've been embarrassed to tell anyone I've been going for counseling. I don't know anyone in my circle of friends that has ever had to go for help like this. It scares me to think of them judging me that I am not trusting You!*

But before I got home, I felt clearly that I was to call Margie and see what she thought about me going for counseling. I feared that someone as together as she was would not approve. My emotions were all over the place. On one hand I thought God was bringing me to a higher level in my walk with Him, and then I feared I was involved in some kind of psychological mumbo-jumbo!

Margie and I were not close, let's-go-to-lunch buddies, but I respected her and trusted her advice. I called her, and we agreed to meet for lunch the next day. I was guarded when we sat down. The last thing I felt like doing was eating, but I was used to going through the motions.

I prayed, *Lord, I don't have anyone else to talk to, so please help me to open my mouth and talk.*

I briefly gave her my emotionless, canned story. I then revealed, "I have been going out of town to a counselor for six weeks. I don't know if I am doing the right thing or not."

I was surprised at Margie's reaction. She gently, ever so gently, like she was diffusing a bomb, said, "I'm so glad you're going to a counselor."

She opened the door wide for me to walk through. She accepted me without judgment. It was clear to me, too, that I had come a long way in six weeks, because I began to open my heart and cautiously talked to her about the lies I believed about myself.

"Margie, I believed those lies all my life. I'm ashamed that it has taken me all this time to recognize how very wrong my thinking has

been. I've been locked in my own private prison and have refused
to believe there was anything wrong with that. I have had my mind
stubbornly made up that I—" I couldn't even continue. It was beginning to sound silly even to me.

Margie's face seemed to glow with compassion. "Lana, you didn't
know any better. God has had to build a firm foundation under you
first. I'm just sorry you've suffered alone all these years."

I smiled at her in amazement. "Rose told me this would happen.
If I'd begin to talk, if I'd begin to risk opening up, I'd find validation
for the first time in my life. Margie, I guess my friends have tried
to reach into my heart, but I've absolutely refused to believe I was
deserving of any kindness at all. Rose told me that I had shut out
the good along with the perceived bad."

By then I was crying. The fact that Margie was interested in what
I had to say overwhelmed me. I surprised myself at how much I'd
opened up to her. But she'd made it so easy. She said, "We need to
continue meeting, Lana. You can't go through this alone. I would also
like to read a couple of the books Rose is recommending to you."

I was on overload. I felt drained and empowered at the same
time. "Thank you so much, Margie. I'm very humbled that you cared
to listen to me ramble." I was going to continue gushing my appre-
ciation when she hugged me.

"Lana, I wish you could see yourself the way I see you and the way
countless others you have touched through the years see you. I've
admired you and your wisdom as long as I've known you. Nothing
you will ever say will change my opinion of you! God is up to something big, and I feel honored that you chose me to talk to."

Rose was pleased when I told her about my visit with Margie. She
advised, "Keep talking, keep talking. Sure, it's scary. But once the
truth is uncovered, you'll be free from a lifetime of lies." Then she
added, "Be patient. Your unhealthy defense mechanisms will slowly
begin to fall away."

"I feel like I still have a huge mountain standing between me and
the rest of the world. The side they look at is different than what I
see. I feel that if you looked at my life on heart monitor, it would be
flatlined."

Rose explained, "One of your main coping mechanisms growing up was, 'I am a non-person.' You didn't have any rationalizing skills as a child to know how to deal with the day-in and day-out suffering you experienced. If you expressed pain, you could be sent away or abandoned again. You had a terrible dilemma!"

She looked intently at me. "You know, Lana, you creatively invented your own reality. All people hurt, feel pain, and have a whole range of emotions. So if you were a nobody, nothing of importance, a non-person, then you didn't have a right to react or feel pain. Those words insulated you from normal human emotions."

Everything she said rang true and yet was too good to be true.

"You beat yourself into submission to this new belief system to avoid the horrendous pain. Whenever you felt terrified, abandoned, abused, or unloved, you fiercely tore yourself down. You showed no mercy to poor little Lana. But beating yourself down caused you to survive!"

I decided to tell her something else. "When I oversee retreats or speak...somewhere...often I receive...thank you cards...I generally hesitate...to...open...them." I could tell I was drifting off and shutting Rose out.

"Lana, wait. I can see you pulling into yourself. Share what you're seeing. Let go of what you're hiding from. Go ahead and release that."

I made myself go back to what I was trying to say. "I can see myself happily walking down my driveway to the mailbox. I take the mail out and begin to sort through it. I can identify thank you cards by their shape and return addresses generally. As soon as I see them, I feel disoriented. I put them on the bottom of the stack of mail."

She asked, "And you've done this many times? Then what happens?"

"I walk back up the driveway in a daze, almost dizzy. I set the thank you notes aside, unopened. Then I have to sit down. But after a couple of days I finally feel guilty for not opening them. They had been kind enough to take time to write them. They may need my acknowledgement for their kindness, so then I open them. But I become so bewildered when someone directs compliments to me."

Rose nodded. "When someone compliments you, it makes no sense to you because you don't know how to respond when someone treats you like a real person. A compliment is confusing because it doesn't match up with your belief system."

Once more, on my ride home I prayed, *Lord, I think I'm beginning to understand. Thank you for Your protection throughout my life. I love You and adore You. Forgive me for not even talking to You about the madness I was living in. I didn't know there was a chance for change. I've always wanted to do Your will. I see more clearly how I kept my emotional turmoil under lock and key and didn't even ask for help from You. But thank You that by Your grace and forgiveness I'm free and becoming more free!*

So that is how it went. I talked, and Rose gave me a reality check of what the truth was. I cried. I didn't laugh until much later in the process. The whole course of talking about the past and facing it was hard.

Sometimes I told Margie, "I think I am ready to quit counseling. I don't think I can face anymore of my past pain."

Margie never stopped encouraging me. "It takes a lot of courage to go forward, but you can do it. The truth is what you are seeking so you can be truly free."

Finally, the web of self-deception I had lived in became clearer to me. The more I soaked up the truth, the freer I became. I began to really see my endless circle of repeated, self-destructive patterns.

As I became honest with myself, I could see the twisted dysfunction I had grown up in. And I also saw how insanely I had fought to stay there. I could see, too, that my need to rescue others was another part of my dysfunction. Rescuing was familiar to me. My whole identity had been wrapped up in caretaking.

Meanwhile, Aglow began publishing support group books, and I ordered them for The Son Shine Shop. I also completed the course to be an Aglow support group leader. I led the first Aglow support group in our area. About seven of us crowded into a small living room. Even though we had different stories, we had similar emotions.

As I was sharing my story, I realized that, like many others, I had been misquoting Scripture. Most people say that the Bible says that the truth will set you free. But John 8:32 actually says, "You will *know* the truth and it will make you free." I explained to the other women, "That's exactly what happened to me! I had to *know* the truth. Once I began to crack the door of my heart for the Holy Spirit's light to penetrate my walled-off exterior, He began to expose the lies I was clinging to. I had believed with all my heart that I was nothing, that I didn't matter, that I didn't belong. I explained how I had refused to open my heart to any possibility that these thoughts were not true."

Another lie I had believed was: The past is the past. Leave it there. But the truth was, it was *not* behind me. It was strangling the very life out of me on a daily basis. I had to receive healing from my past so I could truly be free today.

The lies had to be exposed for me to see the truth clearly.

I had protected myself by withdrawing into my own made-up child world. The famous love chapter in the Bible, 1 Corinthians 13, says, "When I was a child, I spoke as a child, but when I became an adult, I put away childish things" (v. 11). But I did not put away childish things. As a child my beliefs ingeniously protected me from a mental breakdown. As an adult they were leading me into a mental breakdown.

When I ministered, I began to speak on codependency, emotional healing, and boundaries. I ministered to many, like myself, who refused to look at their past and gain healing. When I first began speaking, I told Margie, "Sometimes I go to meetings feeling so broken, I feel like I'm the last person to try to teach on healing from emotional wounds."

Margie always encouraged me, "None of us would ever get up to speak if we had it all together. Life is a journey, and we are being healed and awakened to God's ways daily." She paused and then began again with extreme seriousness. "It's important that we share our journey with others along the way. We are all fellow strugglers in a complex world."

The more I shared my story, the freer I became. As I gained freedom from my past hurts, I could truly be present for the joy of today.

Instead of being disconnected from the world around me, I slowly began to integrate into society. When Helen came in the bookstore,

I focused on opening my heart to her. She came in the shop often and sometimes shared with me her personal problems. She would open the conversations by asking for me to direct her to a book to help her. "I'm looking for a book on anger. Actually, something about rage."

I always gave her guarded support and encouragement. "God has answers for all of our needs." I then would recommend a book and maybe soothing music. Now I felt like I wanted to risk letting my guard down. I was a fellow human being that was struggling with the cares of this life. "Helen, I too have been stressed at times to the point of rage." I saw that she and I made a connection as we exchanged conversation.

I was so amazed! It felt great to be present in the moment. To actually interact about real life. I found that when I opened up about my life, it freed others to open up and be real also. I was absolutely astonished how that worked. My preschool-level social skills were getting better as I began to open up to others.

I did learn quickly that I should not open up to everyone. I went back in my hole when someone judged me or preached at me. But through experimenting with my new understanding of the truth, I became more skilled at recognizing who was safe to talk to and who wasn't.

I bubbled over with this new freedom. I searched for healthy people that I could cautiously have real conversations with. It felt so energizing to gradually bond with people. I liked talking about reality. I didn't like shallow conversation any longer. When I was in social settings, I watched now with an open heart. I watched to see where I could fit into the conversation with my fellow travelers in this journey called life.

I was having lunch with Polly and Faye as we were making plans for a study group that I was going to teach on boundaries. Eventually the conversation drifted off to a sale at Sears. First I watched them eagerly sharing their thoughts and wishes. I thought to myself, *I have something to contribute to this conversation. They do love and respect me, or they wouldn't be asking me to teach a nine-week course for their group.*

Before speaking, I prayed, *Lord, I ask You to teach me step-by-step. I see now what I have missed out on by not establishing healthy relationships.*

"Polly, why don't we all go to Sears together after lunch. That would be fun!" Was that me that said that? Yep, it was, and it felt good and right!

The emerging me spoke at an Aglow retreat and shared about the deception I had lived in. I talked about how I had declared "the past was in the past;" however, I found the truth was that the past was strangling the very life out of me on a day-to-day basis.

Many leaders were there with whom I had worked in the past. I was surprised by their comments: "You've had a dramatic transformation in your personality!" "I always saw you as a spiritual leader, but you were unapproachable." "I just thought you didn't want to be my friend."

Lord, I am so thankful that You are overhauling me. I had lost my identity in my mama's identity. Now You are helping me find my true self. I lost my way, and now I am home. I love being totally Yours.

My recovery is ongoing. When I find myself trying to revert back to my old coping patterns of tearing myself down, I can recognize what I'm doing. *Lord, my choice is to be unhindered from the chains that had me bound. I embrace the truth and resist a lifetime of lies.*

CHAPTER
SIXTEEN

HERE WAS ONE WORD, even after counseling, that always brought pain to my heart. That word was *family*. Every mention of family brought with it the old familiar hurt. Friends would say, "Remember when you were a kid and..." Then they'd proceed to relate some hilarious or poignant family event.

Not me. The only kid-memories I had were of being alone—always, consistently, repeatedly alone. I never knew the nurturing or interaction of family. Over the years people said to me, "You're *just like* a daughter to me." Others said, "You're *just like* a sister to me."

Just like drew a sharp pain and reminder that I really did not have my own family connection. I can only imagine how bizarre it would have sounded if I had told someone how long I'd held on to this childhood pain. But I did hold on to it, fiercely, wanting desperately to let it go, but not knowing how.

I clicked instantly with a woman named Catherine Holden, whom I'd met at Brother Sidney's home the first day I moved to Sulphur. She and her husband, Sam, were very good friends of Sidney and Delores Fontenot. She had that mother look, deep blue eyes, and wavy light brown hair. She was energetic and was bubbling over with the love of the Lord. When Sister Delores introduced me to her, we hugged. Wow, I could smell the gentle scent of flowery bath powder!

I often visited with her at church or the bookstore. She became active in Aglow, and we went to meetings and retreats together. She is an LPN, and when I was sick she actually cared for me.

Catherine had seven children that I knew, being in and out of her house often. She always had room for me, though.

Her husband, Sam, and I had a book connection. He loved reading, and we regularly discussed books, ideas, and authors. I enjoyed running things by him. He was never at a loss for offering suggestions.

Dalton, one of the Holden grandchildren, had always called me Aunt Lana. He called his grandparents Mama-Kate and Daddy-Sam. Michael and I never had any children of our own, but everyone around us knew that our nephew, Dalton, was the love of our lives.

Michael and I both loved being part of the Holden family; so much so that sometimes I introduced Catherine and Sam as my parents. Then I'd walk away with that familiar, lonely pain and tell myself, "You're so silly. You don't really belong to the Holden family at all."

But I would always come back to it, saying in passing, "My brother, Steve; my sister, Laura; my sister, Diane; my brother, Matt, and I are the oldest." I proudly said, "My aunt is the mayor of Iowa, Louisiana."

Then a lady from Sulphur confronted me, "They aren't really your family."

Embarrassed, I floundered around for an explanation. "Well, out of all the foster families I lived in, I've been a part of their family the longest."

At the end of the day, when I laid my head on my pillow, I faced a reality check. I told myself, "Lana, you're not really a Holden, not really a part of their family at all."

Michael and I went to the Holdens' for most holidays, and that is why we were there on that Easter Sunday. Mark, their fourth child, who is an attorney, asked that we all gather in the living room.

Mike and I were just about to sit on the couch next to Mama-Kate when she held up her hand. "No, Mike, you sit over there; Sam is going to sit on the other side of Lana." They had a large sectional couch, and we three—Mama-Kate, Daddy-Sam, and I—in the middle, sat on one side. There was a coffee table in front of us, and Mark sat across from us. He laid some papers on the coffee table in front of me. Everyone in the room watched. Mama-Kate took hold of my hand.

Mark said, "I am going to read a legal document." In an official stentorian voice he began to read:

Affidavit of Adoption. State of Louisiana. Parish of Calcasieu.

Sam Ray Holden Jr. and Catherine Boggs Holden do by these present hereby adopt Susan Arnene Pete Hafner, with all rights, privileges, and legal obligations and consequences flowing therefrom, as if she were born into the family of Sam Ray Holden Jr. and Catherine Boggs Holden on the date of her birth, May 8, 1949.

What on Earth! I struggled to comprehend. *Me? They want to adopt me?* My stomach flip-flopped. Huge tears cascaded down my cheeks. I thought Mama-Kate was going to squeeze my hand off.

"...as if she were born into the family...on the date of her birth!"

I had never heard of such a thing! Could it be that as an adult, I was being legally adopted the same way a baby is adopted? I could hardly believe it!

After Mark read the document, he asked, "Do you each agree to this document?"

I sat there like I was back in the lunchroom in high school the day after being born again. I'd hesitated at the end of the lunch line to make sure I'd not misread their signals. Now sitting in the living room, so many years later, I hesitated, making sure I hadn't misread what was happening.

Dad spoke first, "Yes."

My new mom spoke, "Yes, yes, yes." She was giddy with excitement and anticipation.

Mark asked, "Lana, do you agree to be adopted by Sam and Catherine Holden?" Still in unbelief, I reached over and hugged Mom. "Are you sure?"

"Of course we're sure! We have discussed this as a family. We contacted all of the children. We are sure, but we are just afraid you might say no."

Now I was really crying. "Yes."

Dad said, "Now Michael, as far as we're concerned, all our children's spouses are our children also."

Michael, with his long arms and quick wit, threw open his arms wide and exclaimed, "Daddy!"

Dad then presented me with a big bouquet of red roses! Then as a family we all toasted with sparkling grape juice.

Mom could hardly wait to get to the courthouse to officially register it.

Mom cooks soup for me when I'm sick, sews whatever is needed, and is always doing things for me. So many times I've said, "Mom, thank you so much for helping me."

She always replies, "Honey, that's what moms do for their children."

Dad gives me Valentines candy each year and is the handyman-dad that fixes anything at our house.

The first Thanksgiving after the adoption we spent at my sister Dianne's in Houston. Before Dad asked the blessing, we held hands in a circle, and each one said what he or she was thankful for. When it was my turn, I said, "I'm thankful for my birth parents, who taught me about life; and for my adoptive parents, who taught me about love."

Shortly after the adoption, Mom wrote me this letter:

> My precious Lana,
>
> My jewel, my gem, my daughter! Not many moms get to select a daughter already possessing all the wonderful attributes you exhibit. Because you said yes to God when you were young, He guided you through the trials you had to endure. He saw your potential and claimed you to be His from that time on. When we first met, I had no idea I would ever be able to call you mine. But God had a plan, there, too. And our friendship blossomed and fully bloomed into the sincere, loving relationship that is ours today. I have admired and respected you from the beginning, and that has grown to fruition in the love that we share.

I received you, as mine, already made-to-order, compassionate, caring, serving, always trying to follow Jesus' example.

Others wanted to be your family, but I won the prize!

MUCH LOVE,

YOUR EVER-LOVING MOM

My mother, my family. I still weep over this letter.

EPILOGUE

The Founding of One Touch Awakening, Inc.

I RETIRED FROM THE BOOKSTORE. I limited my speaking opportunities. All my life I had been busy and extremely responsible. Now I was not really interested in being involved in anything else.

Michael and I built a home on the river. I told people I felt I was on perpetual vacation.

I told God, "I feel like I have run my course in this life."

I saw nothing that I wanted to do or that God was asking me to do. I told my friend, "I am a woman of passion; unless I feel it deep in my heart, I am not interested in just occupying my time."

All that changed when my sister, Laura, and I went to Houston to visit with our other sister, Dianne.

The last night we were there, I lay down and snuggled with my pillow I had brought from home. With my hand on my pillow, I said my nighttime prayers and asked God for renewed hope.

I awakened to an unfolding vision that lasted thirty minutes. It so changed me, I would never see the world the same!

The first thing I saw in the vision was a woman lying in a hospital bed. She was partially propped up. She had on a blue-and-white hospital gown. A woman came to visit her at the hospital and gave her a gift containing a pillowcase, a music CD, and a teaching about God visiting with you during the night. On the outside of the package was a greeting card. The greeting card said, "To _____," and then there was a prayer about hope. Under that it read, "I am signing my name below to assure you that prayers are being said especially for you. From _____." Several names were signed on the card.

She handed the gift to the woman in bed and said, "The members of your Sunday School class have each signed their name. We are all praying for you. You are not alone."

The woman then eagerly reached for the package. It was obvious she was reaching for help in this hour of need. She was reaching for hope. She was no longer alone in this trial.

As she opened the gift, the woman said, "This CD is for you to go to sleep by. It will quiet you down and help usher you into a peaceful night's sleep in the presence of God. The pillowcase is your reminder each night that we are praying for you. I want you to know we all gathered around and laid our hands on your pillowcase and each said a prayer for you."

She said, "This is to remind you that as you lay your head on your pillow, prayers are being said especially for you. It is also to remind you that God, your Creator, is with you to minister to you while you are resting."

I knew overwhelmingly that the pillowcase was a lifeline for the woman in bed. It was a lifeline like it had been for my mama. It was a point of contact with people who cared for them and also a tangible connection with God.

I then saw other people in hospitals who were receiving prayer-soaked pillowcase gifts from a friend, a parent, families, organizations, or coworkers.

As I watched, I saw a need to teach people how to be a blessing to others. It wasn't about just taking flowers and leaving. It wasn't just sending a greeting card. It was a powerful impartation from one spirit to another. It wasn't just saying, "God bless you," in a haphazard way but connecting spirit to spirit, imparting the life-changing power of God.

I realized this gift of a pillowcase could be the point of contact. The pillowcase represents the quietest time of the day, when we are in a surrendered state. It is personal, having our aura, our scent. It could provide people with an opportunity for a personal meeting place with God.

The scene switched.

I saw lots of traffic at an intersection of two very busy highways in a large city.

The traffic was traveling north, east, south, and west.

As the cars went by, I saw the people's faces. I saw a wide assortment of people.

Some stared blankly, some were in a hurry, some talked endlessly, some were angry; some had very nice cars, some had clunkers; some were on buses, some were in taxies; some were on motorcycles, some were on bicycles; some were in eighteen-wheelers, some were in pickups.

They were all people created by God and all part of the human race. Except some slept on our pillowcases soaked in prayer, and some didn't. The pillowcases represented an opportunity for these people to have comfort each night, to have a visitation with God each night, to have hope each morning when they awakened.

I saw a movement spreading across the nation as more and more and more people began sleeping on pillowcases that were part of a vast prayer network. I saw it widespread like the "random acts of kindness" and WWJD movements. I lay there reflecting on what I was seeing.

The vision never really faded. It was like I stepped into another realm that others couldn't see. I realized I had not only seen it, but I now was part of it! I stepped into a worldwide movement that was yet to happen.

I shared my vision with my sisters and brother-in-law that morning. I told them with complete confidence, "Everything I have done in the past has prepared me for this!"

I founded a non-profit organization, One Touch Awakening. We distribute pillowcases that are monogrammed with the words *One Touch*. On the inside is a fabric label that says, "One touch from God is greater than all the world can offer." The pillowcases are prayed over by those who give them, prayed for by prayer teams, and prayed for by all of us who handle them. We distribute the pillowcases in Packages of Hope to the homeless, troops, The National Alliance on Mental Illness (NAMI), prisoners reentering society, hospice, the discouraged, the lonely, the hopeless—everyone. Everyone sleeps, and everyone needs hope.

For the people who receive them, these pillowcases are a simple connection with God without anyone preaching to them. No one is telling them how to live their lives. It is strictly an encounter between each person and his or her Creator in the quiet of the night.

All day long God is guiding and inspiring us, but we are so busy in the hustle and bustle of life that it is hard to hear Him clearly. At night when things settle down, we can put on our jammies, bury our heads in our pillows, and listen for His voice. Or we can simply say, "God help me."

The thief on the cross merely said to Jesus, "Remember me", and Jesus responded to his heart's cry.

People may not go to church or may not have anyone who talks to them about God, but with the One Touch pillowcase they now have a connection—a major connection to a diligent, serious, God-loving prayer network.

We also distribute mosquito nets to Africa, where people can't sleep for fear of malaria from mosquitoes. Each mosquito net distributed in Africa is accompanied by a poster to hang on their wall that says:

> One touch from God is greater than all the world can offer.
> Know that the presence of the Lord God, your Creator, is with
>   you.
> You can be assured that when you lay your head to rest
> under your One Touch mosquito net, prayers are being said
>   for you!

We also distribute One Touch Snuggle Pillows® that are a travel pillow and pillowcase for children. The booklet that accompanies it reads, "If someone makes you mad during the day or hurts your feelings, this is your secret meeting place with God!"

Truly, every experience I have had in my life has prepared me for this worldwide awakening!

Today One Touch Awakening partners with many organizations. But the biggest partnership we have made, and continue to make, is with each individual who has the opportunity to connect with God in the privacy of his or her own home, or under starry skies, or in the sleeper cab of an eighteen-wheeler, or wherever.

We are partners with each individual without fanfare or showmanship.

Our mission is to encourage a personal encounter with our Creator and to remind everyone: one touch from God is greater than all the world can offer!

TO CONTACT
THE AUTHOR

One Touch Awakening, Inc.
P.O. Box 16838
Lake Charles, LA 70615
(337) 529-0858
www.OneTouchAwakening.org

**All resources including, One Touch Pillowcases
and One Touch Snuggle Pillows, are available at
the above address.**